Own It, Earn It, Build It

The Millionaire Mindset for Women

By Amulya Mishra

Amulya Mishra is a proficient author and banking specialist with a profound interest in economic theory and storytelling. Amulya's work is grounded on a robust academic and practical foundation, since he possesses an MBA in Banking and Finance, a graduate degree in Accounting, and other banking certifications.

Amulya was born and nurtured in Patna, and his journey has been characterized by discipline, curiosity, and creativity. His works, encompassing both fiction and non-fiction, exemplify his extensive intellect and insatiable curiosity. His non-fiction writings, such as "Bond: A Barometer of the Economy" and his analysis of the G20 Presidency, illustrate his capacity to distill complex topics into engaging narratives, encompassing issues ranging from the intricacies of cryptocurrencies to the dynamics of international financial instruments.

His conceived universes, meanwhile, are equally enthralling. His gripping horror novel "Mirror Mirror Mirror" showcases a chilling imagination, while his forthcoming work "Superpower 2050" appears to be a formidable geopolitical analysis.

In staying soft in hard times he showcases depthness.

Amulya has been writing for as long as he can recall and is inherently a writer. He perceives writing as a vocation that intertwines facts and emotions, reason and wonder, rather than simply a craft.

This piece signifies yet another step in his evolving literary career. Amulya asserts that his words exert a profound and substantial influence on you, irrespective of your purpose for being here—be it inspiration, exhilaration, or reflection. I value your support of him on this trip, and I trust this endeavor will offer you pleasure and heightened engagement.

DISCLAIMER

This book is a non-fiction work aimed at elucidating the changing dynamics of global banking and finance. Recent years have witnessed significant changes in geopolitics, technology, and economic theory, necessitating a reassessment of conventional financial systems. These transformations—driven partly by regional tensions, digital disruption, and the advent of artificial intelligence—have elicited both apprehensions and opportunities for the future.

This book refrains from endorsing any sort of prejudice or bias toward persons, institutions, or nations. It seeks to provide insights into the possible trajectories of global finance by 2050. In this era of hyper-connectivity, the significance of technical ethics, economic inclusiveness, and human-centric innovation is paramount.

All views expressed below are exclusively those of the author and aim to stimulate critical analysis and informed dialogue. The opinions expressed do not represent the official position of financial institutions or regulatory authorities.

———————————————————————

Disclaimer on Empowerment

The purpose of this book is to encourage, mentor, and uplift aspirational women who are prepared to take charge of their financial destiny. Research, experience, and a passion for enabling women to succeed financially, personally, and professionally serve as the foundation for the concepts, tactics, and mentality changes discussed here.

Please be aware, nevertheless, that this does not replace expert, legal, or financial advice. Each woman's journey is different. The information presented here is not intended to ensure outcomes, but rather to inspire hope and confidence.

When making significant decisions, you are advised to get advice from a qualified financial advisor, business strategist, or legal specialist. Make use of your team, your power, and your instincts.

Individual decisions are beyond the control of the author and publisher, and we hope you will make them with the same audacious goal that led you to this book.

This is about rising, not simply about reading. You're capable.

I did not write this book to provide you a secret recipe.
I wrote it because I really believe that women were never intended to play small whether it came to their voice, their influence, or their financial resources.
We've been instructed to wait our turn for far too long. to make us less brilliant. to expect that the system will change for us, ask for less, and accept less.
The fact is, however, that you can accumulate riches without authorization.
You don't have to be flawless.
All you have to do is begin.
Late nights, audacious dreams, inner struggles, and ferocious discussions with women who

were tired of waiting gave rise to Own It, Earn It, Build It. Women like you—creators, leaders, visionaries, and warriors—who secretly believe they were destined for more. This book serves as a guide for overcoming scarcity, gaining self-assurance, and creating a life full of autonomy, meaning, and unreserved achievement.

I wrote this with my mother's strength and wisdom in mind. She demonstrated to me that we are more powerful than we may have thought by her deeds rather than her words. She demonstrated to me that no challenge is too big to conquer and that our value is not determined by the constraints of the outside world. Her strength, grace, and tenacity served as the inspiration for my book and served as a constant reminder to me that women like us should succeed.

It's not about get-rich-quick foolishness or hustling mentality. It's about financial, emotional, and mental change.
This book is your call to rise, whether you're launching a company, moving up the corporate ladder, recovering from setbacks, or just wanting more. to be aware of your value. to create enduring riches.

Each chapter serves as a map and a mirror, reflecting your current self and pointing you in the direction of your future self.
You read more than simply this book.
You enter it.
And the world changes when you do.

Thus, inhale deeply and prepare yourself.
Because this is where your millionaire attitude begins.
With strength and intent,
[Amulya]

ACKNOWLEDGEMENTS

I would like to express my deepest gratitude to my family, especially my wife, Sheetal, whose unwavering love and support have been my strength throughout the writing of this book. Her encouragement during moments of doubt gave me the clarity and determination to keep moving forward.

To my beloved parents—my first teachers and my lifelong inspiration—thank you for your sacrifices, wisdom, and the values you instilled in me. Your blessings and faith in my journey have guided me every step of the way.

I also wish to thank my colleagues and peers in the banking and financial sector, especially those in Goa, who fostered an environment that allowed ideas to flourish and this work to take shape.

Spiritually, I bow in gratitude to the divine presence that has illuminated my path during challenging times. I offer humble thanks to Haji Ali Dargah for the strength and serenity I have found there, to Shirdi Sai Baba for continuous guidance, and to all the divine forces who watched over me throughout this journey. Their blessings have been a silent but powerful force behind this book.

This work is also a result of years of reflection, learning, and persistent inquiry. I thank all my teachers and professors who nurtured my curiosity and gave me the tools to think critically and write meaningfully.

Above all, I thank the Almighty for the gift of life, knowledge, and purpose. May this book serve its readers well and contribute to a future shaped by wisdom, innovation, and integrity.

Own It, Earn It, Build It: The Millionaire Mindet for Women

Are you bored playing little, making less money, and waiting for permission to climb?

It's time to turn the script around—and The Millionaire Mindet for Women demonstrates just how.

For the woman who believes she is meant for more, this inspiring, no-fluff manual is Whether your firm is just getting started, you are climbing the job ladder, or you are ready to take back your financial power, this book offers the skills, mentality changes, and aggressive plans to transform your vision into lifetime riches.

Inside you will discover how to:

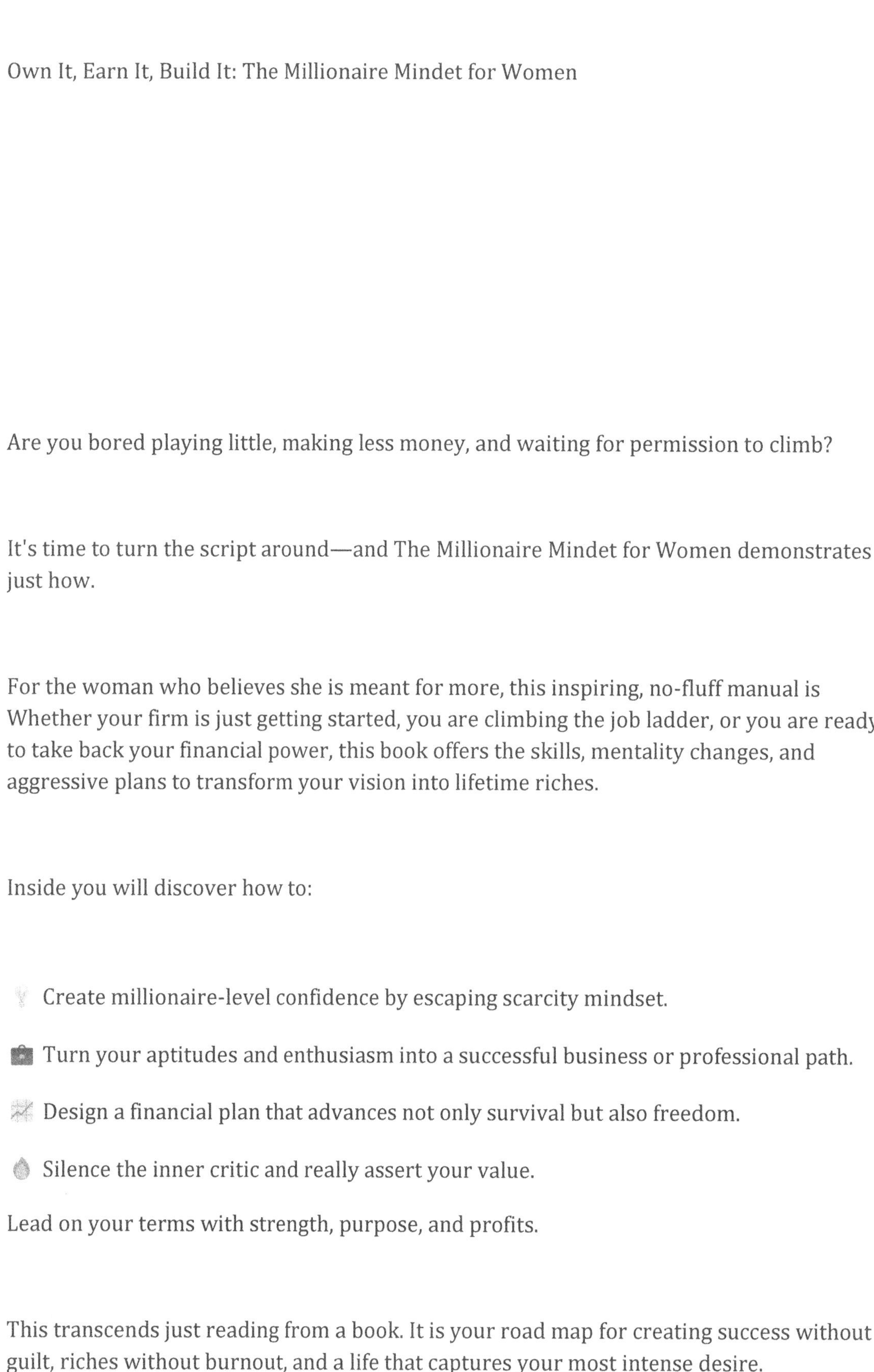

Create millionaire-level confidence by escaping scarcity mindset.

Turn your aptitudes and enthusiasm into a successful business or professional path.

Design a financial plan that advances not only survival but also freedom.

Silence the inner critic and really assert your value.

Lead on your terms with strength, purpose, and profits.

This transcends just reading from a book. It is your road map for creating success without guilt, riches without burnout, and a life that captures your most intense desire.

You are not here trying to fit in. Here you are to create your legacy.

Possess it. Create it.

You were not born small player. You were meant to be rising.

Your road map to own value, create genuine wealth, and rewrite your financial story—on your own terms—the Millionaire Mindet for Women.

This book, full of strong attitude changes, doable financial plans, and unreserved confidence, is for driven women determined to turn their ideas into success.

Hold it. Learn it. Develop it. Your millionaire attitude begins now.

Good! Start writing the first few chapters by first outlining The Millionaire Mindet for Women: Own It, Earn It, Build It. This will lay a solid basis for your novel and direct the idea flow.

Outline of Chapters:

Chapter 1: The Millionaire Mindet—where It All Starts

The power of perspective: Why should one start with building wealth?

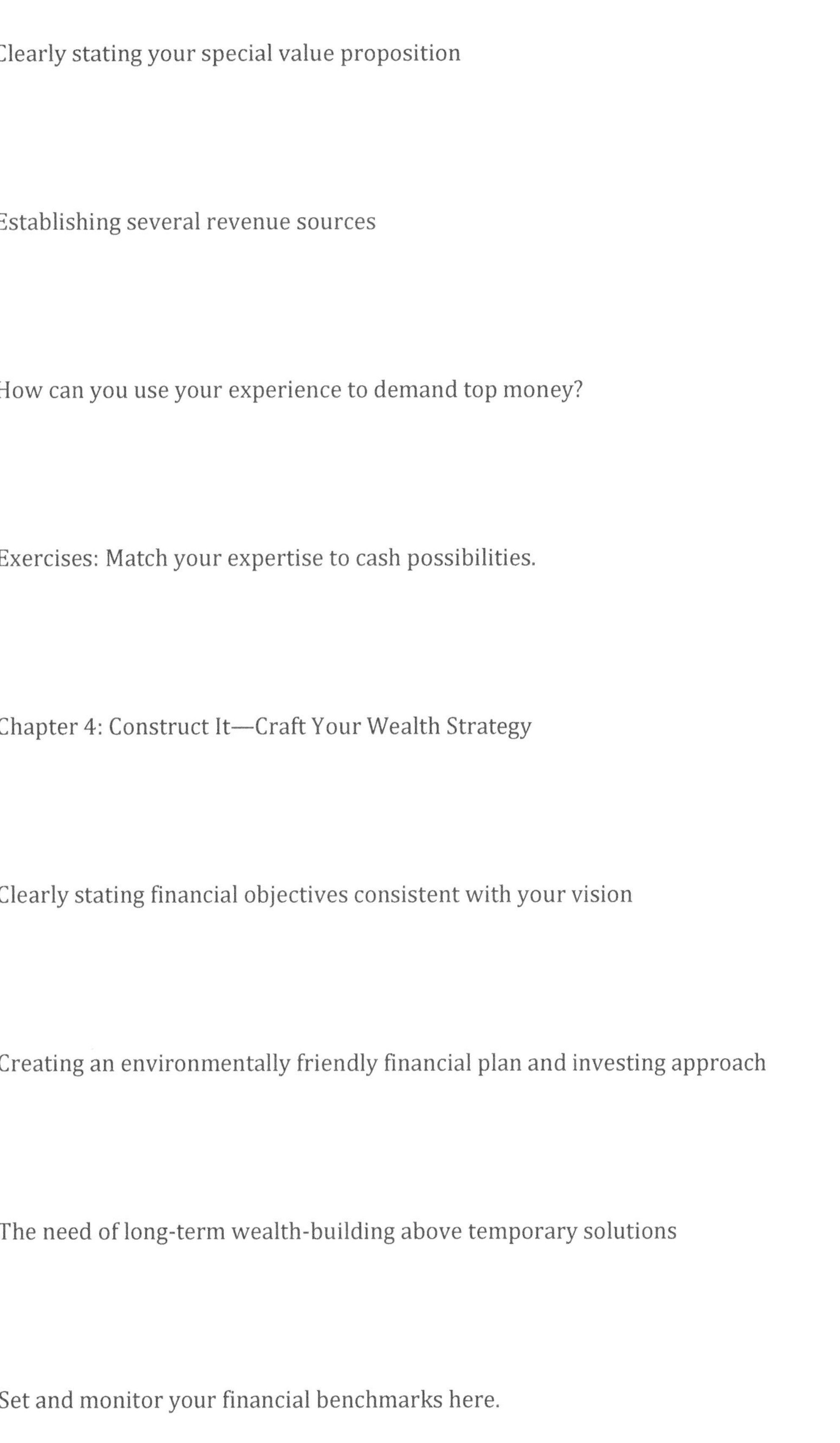

Clearly stating your special value proposition

Establishing several revenue sources

How can you use your experience to demand top money?

Exercises: Match your expertise to cash possibilities.

Chapter 4: Construct It—Craft Your Wealth Strategy

Clearly stating financial objectives consistent with your vision

Creating an environmentally friendly financial plan and investing approach

The need of long-term wealth-building above temporary solutions

Set and monitor your financial benchmarks here.

Chapter 5: Empowerment in Action—Overcoming Doubt and Fear

Getting beyond imposter syndrome and fear of failing.

How well motivated and focused successful women remain?

turning obstacles into possibilities

Exercises: Developing resilience and seeing success visually

Chapter 6: Building a Life of Freedom—Wealth Beyond Money

The part passion and purpose play in creating prosperity.

How to strike a mix between pleasure and fulfillment and riches?

Identifying and honoring turning points on the path.

How do you stay long-term in a millionaire's mindset?

Maintaining humility and returning favor: How may riches help others?

Exercises: Considering your path and objectives going forward

First chapter: The millionaire attitude—where it all starts

Beginning:

You have to first rethink money if you want to create wealth. Your financial future is based on your attitude; so, whatever you do going forward is molded by the ideas you have on your capacity to succeed. This chapter will dissect the ideas of the millionaire attitude, how to go beyond mental obstacles, and why embracing this attitude is non-negotiable for building long-lasting wealth.

The power of perspective:

Though this is anchored in actual psychology, we have all heard the adage, "What you think, you become." It is not only a motivating quote. Your actions produce your results; your thoughts help you to shape them. You will make decisions consistent with those views if you believe you do not deserve riches or that money is beyond your reach. On the other hand, if you feel you are qualified for financial success will start to behave boldly and with empowerment that reflects that confidence.

Abundance versus scarcity:

Changing from a scarcity to an abundance mindset is fundamental in the millionaire attitude. A scarcity mindset holds that resources—money, time, possibilities—are few, which causes tension, anxiety, and worry and drives rivalry. Conversely, an abundant mentality sees that success is not a zero-sum game and that there is more than enough for everyone. Operating from a place of abundance draws possibilities, creativity, and expansion.

Overcoming Restrained Ideas:

Often rooted in childhood or prior events, limited ideas about money can be quite strong. Typical limiting beliefs are:

"I'm not strong with money."

"Wealth is for other people, not folks like me."

"Desiring money is greedy."

Admitting these ideas is the first step in conquering them. Once you identify the tales you have been telling yourself, you can rework them into inspiring ideas like

"I am financially strong and able of producing riches."

"I will make financial success my reality; I deserve it."

"Wealth is a tool that helps me to live my fullest life."

Exercise: Determine Your Financial Viewpoint

Spend some time considering how you now view money.

List any ideas or words that immediately strike you regarding money.

Are these ideas helping you?

List the ideas that either empower or keep you back.

Refine your ideas.

Create fresh sets of empowering ideas about money. These ideas should complement the lady you are growing to be.

You mentioned:

Continually write.

 observed:

Undoubtedly! Let's keep developing Chapter 1 using the concepts forward.

Chapter 1 (Continued) The Millionaire Mindset—Where It All Starts

From Scarcity to Abundance of Thought

Your millionaire mindset is based on the change from scarcity to abundance. In a society that sometimes stresses constraints, it's tempting to adopt a "there's not enough"—not enough time, not enough money, not enough resource attitude. This kind of thinking keeps you in survival mode, in which case you are always running to catch up. Like driving with the brakes on.

Conversely, the secret to release the financial freedom you are yearning is abundant thinking. It's not about discounting the difficulties; rather, it's about changing your perspective so that, should you be ready to believe it and act, you will find countless chances. By means of abundance thinking, one can transcend fear and enter possibilities, therefore opening the path for wealth.

Start changing your perspective with these ideas:

Celebrate the achievements of others as a mirror of what is feasible for you instead of becoming jealously or competitive.

Change your perspective: Reword any idea of shortage you come across. Say, "How can I make this work?" instead of "I can't afford this."

Spend time daily seeing the countless opportunities for your life. See your riches rising, your influence widening, and your confidence skyrocketing.

Remember: Abundance is about opening your mind to the countless opportunities in every circumstance rather than only about having more money.

Developing a Wealth-First Attitude

Giving riches top priority in your life is among the most potent decisions you can make. Many women are taught to put family, friends, coworkers first—above their own financial situation. Starting to view your financial situation as a top concern will help you to create long-term wealth.

This is not selfish; rather, it's realizing that when you look after your financial circumstances, you can also look after people close by. Imagine being able to donate freely, invest in your future, and exercise your freedom to make decisions free from continual financial concern. That begins with seeing your financial development as important.

The Mindset of a Millionaire: In Action

Results will show up once you start working on changing your views and behavior. Though acquiring the millionaire mindset is a journey rather than a destination, you shouldn't expect things to happen overnight. Here are some doable daily strategies to support your fresh perspective:

Effective women begin their mornings with purpose. With affirmations, goal planning, and visualizing achievement, set the tone for your day. Whether it's reading, journaling, or meditation, design a morning ritual fit for your path toward wealth-building.

Surround yourself with success; your development depends much on the people you interact with. Maintaining your millionaire attitude will be challenging if you surround folks who discuss how difficult money is to acquire or who lack drive for more. Look for a group of like-minded ladies encouraging one another toward their aspirations.

Mind Your Words: Check the language you employ. Out are words like "broke," "struggling," or "can't afford it." Rather, start speaking in motivating words consistent with your financial objectives. Say, "I'm building wealth" or "I am financially abundant." Words have power; they help to define your reality.

Exercise: Develop Your Millionaire Mindset

Make a List of Limiting Beliefs.

List your opinions on success and money. Tell yourself truthfully; then, find which of these ideas stem from lack and fear.

Challenge Your Views:

Ask yourself, for every belief: Where did this originate? Indeed? Is it providing me with what? Refine every belief then into a positive, inspiring declaration. If you have always thought, for instance, "I can't save money," change it to "I am learning how to save and invest wisely."

Create Your Affirmations for Wealth:

Create five affirmations fit for the millionaire attitude. These should be tailored to your objectives, positive, present tense. As a result:

"I deserve success and fortune."

"My financial future is clear and expanding."

"I am a strong, income-generating woman."

Every day repeat these affirmations to start reprogramming your subconscious thinking.

Your mindset determines the road map to victory.

Changing your perspective marks one straightforward, strong step toward financial freedom. Your money does not come about by accident. It is the direct outcome of your perspective, ideas, beliefs, and behavior grounded on those ideas.

We have built the basis for your millionaire attitude in this chapter. You are already headed toward riches and success by adopting abundance thinking, conquering limiting ideas, and matching your daily activities with your financial objectives. Recall that improvement is more important than perfection. Keep showing up for yourself; your attitude will change your financial path.

Review of Chapter 1: Essential Learnings

The most effective weapon you have to create money is your attitude.

To open possibilities, move from scarcity to abundance mentality.

Give your financial situation top attention since focusing wealth will enable you to serve others.

Reinforce your millionaire attitude by means of regular routines, empowering language, and a loving community.

What comes next?

The next stage—owning your worth and confidence—will be covered in Chapter 2. Lack confidence and even the best chances could pass through your hands. We will look at ways to create your impact in the world and honestly claim your value.

wonderful! Let's next start Chapter 2: Own It—Claim Your Worth and Confidence.

Chapter 2: Own It— Claim Your Confidence and Worth

Title: Introduction

The ability of a woman to recognize her value is among the most effective weapons she possesses. Often discounting their value or waiting for outside reinforcement, many women battle with feeling like they deserve success, money, or respect. You have to stand tall and boldly assert your value if you are to really create money and power. This chapter will help you to develop the self-confidence and assurance required to not only acknowledge your worth but also to demand it in all spheres of your life.

Why Owning Your Worth Is Not Negotiable

If you don't believe you're worth it, you cannot create money. Too often, women minimize their abilities, successes, and contributions, instead caving in to others rather than claiming their own triumphs. You reduce your chances to draw in possibilities and negotiate for the things you really deserve when you fail to value yourself.

Owning your value is about appreciating your value as a person, professional, and as someone who has the right to lead a life of financial abundance—not only about knowing your talents.

Within the realm of wealth-building, confidence is absolutely vital. Whether your negotiations are for a raise, a new job, or investments, your confidence will let people know you are exactly what they need. Others will follow suit when you arrive with unreserved confidence.

The Relation of Confidence-Value

Unquestionably, confidence and value are connected. You will more boldly negotiate possibilities, advocate your needs, and challenge limits the more you believe in your value. Confidence is magnetic; it attracts possibilities to you and people. Still, developing this confidence calls for constant effort and deliberate intent.

These strategies help you develop confidence in your value:

Develop Your Self-Reflection Skills

One great method for realizing your achievements and areas of strength is self-reflection. Spend some time celebrating past achievements—big and small—that you had. Whether it's a promotion, a project you turned in successfully, or just getting through a difficult period, appreciating your successes helps you to grow confident.

See Your Success Visualize

Effective women in many fields have a strong tool for visualization. Spend daily picturing your objectives—that is, whether they are meeting a certain financial target, finding a dream career, or establishing yourself as a respected subject-matter expert. Visualization helps you to feel real and reachable for your success, hence increasing confidence.

Celebrate Your Individuality

Every woman boasts a different set of abilities, knowledge, and experience. Your superpower makes you unique. Celebrate your unique quality. Own those strengths— creativity, work ethic, or interpersonal skills—whatever they may be. The first step in being a successful, confident woman is learning to feel good in your own skin.

How Can One Start to Value Themself?

"I own my worth," is one thing to say; another is to live it. You must exercise your worth in daily life if you are really to claim it. You might start like this:

Establish Limits

Letting others use you is one of the first indicators you're not claiming your value. Maintaining your time, energy, and self-respect in both personal and professional life depends on you setting limits. Clearly defining what is acceptable and unacceptable helps you to save your energy and express your value.

Work on Your Value Negotiations

Never back off from bargaining for what you deserve whether it's for a raise, pricing your services, or a contract. Key are study and preparation. Know your value; know the market value of your good or ability; and don't hesitate to seek for it. The worst that may happen is you say "no"—but, when you approach negotiations with confidence, the response will most usually be "yes".

Get Over Your Apologizing for Your Success

Women especially are indoctrinated to minimize their achievements in order to avoid coming out as haughty or arrogant. Apologies are no longer needed. Celebrate your success and boldly share it. Owning your achievements is about appreciating the diligence, will, and fortitude required to reach your objectives—not about haughtiness.

Conquering the Anxiety of Evaluation

The fear of judgment is a big obstacle in the path of claiming your value. Many women worry about coming across as overly ambitious, too aggressive, or too preoccupied with their own success. Often resulting from society indoctrination, where women are expected to be modest and self-sacrificing, this anxiety results from

Still, fear of criticism will only prevent you from realizing your own best potential. To overcome this, one must:

Accept that certain people will judge you no matter what you do. That is indeed true. But your worth should not be defined by judgment.

Center on your goal. Keep your attention on your goal and the reasons for your initial money development activities. You will be less influenced by others' ideas the more in line your goal is.

Surround yourself with encouraging individuals; spend time with those who help you to realize your vision. Their assistance will assist to silence the negative voices.

The Worth Evaluation: Exercise

Spend some time considering how valuable you now see yourself to be. Think about how you show up in different spheres of your life and where you might be undervaluing yourself.

Point up places where you shrink.

List times when you have neglected to own your value, whether it's in personal relationships or in asking for what you deserve at work.

Reword those circumstances.:

Now, if you were completely secure in your value, list how you would handle those circumstances. In what way would you seek more? You would define what limits?

Affirm your value.

Make a list of words that support your worth in both personal and business spheres. For instance:

"I contribute special worth to every project I work on."

"I am due pay for my knowledge and abilities."

"I am deserving of financial and success abundance."

Developing Your Confidence via Behavior

Action builds confidence. Your confidence will grow as you more actively embrace your power and declare your value. Take chances, advocate, and write your own story. As you keep learning to value yourself, you will find that you not only start to feel more confident but also draw the chances and people who fit your higher sense of value.

Chapter 2 Review: Essential Learning Points

Confidence is absolutely vital. Your capacity to boldly assert your value will directly affect both your personal and financial success.

Create limits to guard your time, money, and energy.

Bargain for what you are worth; don't hesitate to demand more.

Stop running from your success; own it and grow to be proud of it.

Take action; regular action helps one develop confidence. You will believe your worth more the more you practice owning it.

What comes next?

We will explore the value of earning it in Chapter 3—how to use your talents and get actual, cash money. This chapter will enable you to optimize your earning potential whether you are negotiating a salary raise or generating a new income source.

Nice! Next up is Chapter 3: Earn It—Unlocking Your Full Earning Potential.

Chapter 3: Unlock Your Full Earning Potential

Beginning:

Making money in the modern world is about working smarter rather than only harder. You must release your entire earning capacity if you want to really create riches and assert financial freedom. This chapter will show you how to find possibilities, use your abilities, and develop a mindset that draws financial wealth so that you may deliberately increase your income. This chapter offers a road map for producing more money on your terms whether your business is expanding, you are climbing the corporate ladder, or you are investigating side projects.

The Authority of a Developed Mindset

You should have the correct attitude before starting useful actions to raise your revenue. A growth mindset is the conviction that, with committed effort, your intelligence, talents, and abilities can be developed. Women who have a growth mindset see that every event presents a chance for learning and development and that their earning potential is unbounded.

Conversely, a rigid perspective reduces your possibilities. It keeps you back by persuading you that all you have to work with is your present situation or level of ability. Your attitude to earning changes from one of constraint to one of possibilities when you feel you can progress.

To develop a growth mentality, consider:

How might I pick up fresh knowledge or abilities to raise my earning potential?

Where may I find chances for development even in demanding circumstances?

From whom accomplished women or mentors should I draw lessons?

One could say: Finding Your Earning Prospects

Finding where and how you might create money is one of the first steps toward releasing your earning potential. Although many women follow the conventional path—that of pursuing a full-time job—there are many other methods to raise your income. The secret is to look for chances fit your background, skills, and areas of strength and passion.

The path of employment:

If you work, you should always be sure your present position is allowing you to maximize your income potential.

Don't wait for your company to offer you a raise or promotion; negotiate one. Ask for it yourself first. Listing your successes and accomplishments can help you to create a strong case. Remember in negotiations that your worth to the business counts more than just your demand for additional money.

Often women are reluctant to apply for higher roles because they believe they are not "ready" for the post or because of fear of rejection. The fact is, though, women often undersell themselves. If you have the qualifications, apply for those better-paying jobs and leap forward.

The path of entrepreneurship:

Another excellent approach to release income potential is launching your own side project or company. Here is the rationale:

Unlike conventional employment whereby your pay is set, entrepreneurship lets you scale your income depending on the level of effort you commit.

Running your own company lets you manage your hours, workload, and pricing.

Here are some ideas should you be unsure about where to begin:

Whether your work is in writing, design, consulting, or photography, freelancing gives you control over your income potential.

From e-commerce to developing online courses, you can investigate many online business strategies.

Real Estate: Should you have a talent for real estate, investments in this field could be a great means of wealth creation.

The Course of Investment:

Investments provide even another route for increasing your riches. Although this isn't a quick way to make money, over time this long-term approach can yield notable profits.

First, educate yourself on:

Stock market investments pose hazards even if they can offer great returns. Learn about the workings of the market, then give some thought to consulting a financial adviser.

Investing in real estate can either provide passive income from rental properties or profitably sell real estate as it increases value over time.

Though it comes with great danger, cryptocurrencies provide a somewhat fresh approach for the most adventurous investor to increase riches.

two. Using Your Skills to Boost Your Pay-Scale

Leveraging your skills is crucial regardless of the path you follow to increase income. It's not only about working harder but also about applying your already acquired talents in more clever ways.

Which of your skills are marketable?

Consider your inherent aptitudes or your years of experience in which you have become quite competent. Are you outstanding in marketing, writing, organizing, speaking, team leadership, or project management? Are you very adept in handling relationships or problem-solving?

List your five strongest abilities and think about how you might use them to increase your income. Consider:

If you write really well, you might launch a blog or work as a content writer freelancer.

If you are a natural leader, you can investigate project management or perhaps launch your own coaching company.

Grow Your Capacity

Having a talent does not mean you cannot develop it just because it is natural. Search for strategies to always improve your knowledge. Great strategies to keep competitive in your field are online courses, seminars, and certifications. Your pricing for your services will increase as you learn more.

Three: Creating Many Income Streams

Establishing several income sources is one of the best ways for ladies trying to accumulate fortune. Particularly in unpredictable economic times, depending just on one source of income might be dangerous. By diversifying your income, you provide yourself the freedom to grow wealth and weather financial difficulties at the same time.

Strategies for Creating Multiple Income Sources:

Starting a side project—such as freelancing or product sales—can be a fantastic way to generate extra cash.

Invest in real estate;, should you be a rental property owner, it presents a consistent source of revenue.

Create digital items (such as e-books, printables, or courses) and market them online if you have a special talent, say graphic design or writing.

For 4. Use Your Money Managers Strategically

You should learn good financial management when you begin to make more. Wealth-building is about preserving and expanding what you already have, not only about making more. Here's how you deliberately handle your money:

Set away some of your income for savings and investing. Key to long-term wealth growth are an emergency fund and future-oriented investing.

Track Your Spending: See how you spend. Track your expenses and search for places you might cut back on.

Live Below Your Means: You shouldn't spend more simply because you start making more. Keep to a budget that lets you routinely save and invest.

Chapter 3 Review: Important Learnings

Cultivate a growth attitude to release almost limitless income potential.

Find chances for more income—through investments, side projects, or your employment.

Use your particular abilities to demand what you are worth and add value to the market.

Establish several revenue sources to gradually provide financial stability and riches.

Manage your money strategically to retain and increase your wealth.

What comes next?

In Chapter 4, we will concentrate on how to create it—how to use the revenue you are making to generate long-term wealth. Deeply exploring the value of investing, financial management, and developing sustainable wealth-building practices will be the focus of this chapter.

Nice! Let us now turn now to Chapter 4: Build It—Transform Income into Lasting Wealth.

Chapter 4: Create Lasting Wealth from Income

Beginning:

Making money is merely the beginning toward riches. You must concentrate on how to develop and protect wealth over time if you are to really establish financial freedom and stability. The techniques that will enable you to increase your wealth, make wise financial decisions, and make sure your money serves you long after you get it will be covered in this chapter. It's about building a financial ecosystem whereby your income increases, your investments flourish, and your wealth multiplies.

The Value of Funding Your Future

Investing is one of the main differences separating those who just make money from those who create wealth. Investing is the process by which a wage into long-term riches. Simply saving money in a bank account lets your money lose value against inflation and prevents growth of your wealth. But when you invest, you give your money opportunity to work for you.

Investing is for everyone who wants to systematically increase their money, not only for the wealthy or those with experience in finance. Early, even small investments made by you will eventually help you to create riches. Compound interest—where the rewards on your investments create more returns—will help you more the earlier you start.

One is 1. Recognizing Compounding's Power

Often referred to as the "eighth wonder of the world," compound interest is defined as the result of adding earned interest on an investment to the principal amount, therefore determining future interest based on the increased total. This produces a snowball effect over time whereby your returns quicken and exponential growth results.

For instance, in the first year you will make $70 if you invest $1,000 at a 7% annual return. Your $1,070 will make interest in the second year, producing $74.90. The compounding power increases with increasing length of investment for your money.

The main lesson is beginning to invest today. If you are diligent and patient, even little amounts can add up really significantly.

2. Creating Money from Investments

You have many options for investing your money. Your objectives, risk tolerance, and timeframe will determine your appropriate investing plan. For ladies who are committed to accumulate wealth, let's dissect the most often occurring forms of investing.

Investments in Stock Markets

Although the stock market comes with risk, it provides among the best possible returns on investment. Stocks are ownership interests in businesses; so, when those businesses do well, their stocks also do.

Buying individual stocks allows you to invest straight in particular businesses. Still, since stock values are erratic, this calls more study and may be riskier.

Designed to follow a market index, such as the S&P 500, Index Funds and ETFs—Exchange-Traded Funds—are collections of stocks or bonds. Investing in index funds or ETFs offers diversification, therefore lowering the risk of your portfolio of investments.

Real Estate Investments

One tangible asset that can offer cash flow through rental income as well as appreciation—value growth—is real estate. For long-term wealth creation, many women discover that real estate is the best investment available. Real estate provides various benefits whether your purchase is a holiday rental, business space, or house:

Appreciation: Property values rise with time, which would let you profitably sell them.

Investing in rental homes will allow you monthly rent payments to create passive income.

Real estate purchases include tax benefits including deductions on mortgage interest and depreciation.

Although real estate calls for an initial outlay, it may be a great vehicle for creating long-term wealth.

bonds

Bonds are loans you provide governments or businesses in return for interest payments. Though they offer lesser returns, they are usually less dangerous than stocks. Women who wish to preserve cash while keeping a consistent income source could find bonds to be a good choice.

Corporate bonds, issued by businesses, have more risk but higher interest rates.

Considered a fantastic choice for cautious investors, municipal bonds—issued by local governments—often tax-free and lower-risk.

Considered among the safest kind of bonds, government bonds are issued by federal governments.

Group Funds

From many investors, mutual funds aggregate funds to purchase a diversified portfolio of stocks, bonds, or other assets. Professionals oversee these money, thus they are a fantastic choice for those who want a hands-off attitude to investing. They offer diversity, therefore distributing risk.

Third: Making a Long-Term Financial Strategy

Creating wealth requires a strategy more than just investing. A well-considered financial plan will enable you to create goals, monitor your development, and keep on target. A financial strategy comprises

Track your income and expenses to practice budgeting. Make sure you routinely save and invest a fraction of your salary.

Clearly state the definition of financial success for you. Are you hoping to retire early? By a given age, amass a certain level of wealth? Your financial selections will reflect your ambitions.

Eliminating high-interest debt is an absolutely vital first step toward building wealth. Once debt is paid off, more of your income is free for savings and investments.

Having three to six months of living expenses saved aside in an emergency fund is really vital. This offers both financial safety net and mental calm.

Verify your sufficient insurance level. This covers life insurance, health insurance, and—if relevant—disabled insurance.

Making and following a financial plan will enable you to keep concentrated on your long-term objectives for wealth-building.

4. Maintaining Wealth: Guarding What You Created

You have to guard your wealth once you have it. Preserving wealth is future planning, risk management, and asset protection. These are some essential tactics:

Make sure you have a will, trust, or estate plan in place to guarantee your wealth passes on in line with your intentions. Additionally helping to lower estate taxes is this.

Don't lay all of your eggs in one basket; diversify. To lower risk, divide your assets—stocks, bonds, real estate, etc.—among several classes.

Think on how you might guard your possessions from creditors, lawsuits, or other hazards. This can call for using insurance policies or building legal entities like limited liability organizations, or LLCs.

As vital as money production is preservation of wealth. By acting to protect your money, you make sure it keeps expanding and offers your family and yourself financial stability.

Chapter 4 Review: Important Notes

Invest early and regularly to use compounding's ability to grow wealth.

To reduce risk, mix your assets—stocks, bonds, real estate, and other items.

Plan your finances including debt management, emergency savings, budgeting, and goal-setting.

Use asset protection techniques, diversification, and estate planning to guard your fortune.

What's Next?

The last stage in the wealth-building process—getting economic power—will be covered in Chapter 5. You will discover how to maximize your financial resources to influence your life, your neighborhood, and the surroundings more broadly.

Write these chapters with well-known women's persomalies then turn to chapter five.

 stated:

Surely! Chapter 4: Build It — Turning Income into Lasting Wealth should feature some well-known female celebrities. By doing this, we may learn from actual women who have perfected financial independence and wealth-building and share their knowledge and ideas all through the chapter.

Chapter 4: Create It - Convert Income into Lasting Wealth

Title: Introduction

Making money is merely the beginning toward riches. You must concentrate on how to develop and protect wealth over time if you are to really establish financial freedom and stability. The techniques that will enable you to increase your wealth, make wise financial decisions, and make sure your money serves you long after you get it will be covered in this chapter. It's about building a financial ecosystem whereby your money multiplies, your investments flourish, and your income rises. And we will use the travels of successful women who have mastered wealth-building to help to clarify the road forward.

The Value of Funding Your Future

Investing is one of the main differences separating those who just make money from those who create wealth. Investing is the process by which a wage into long-term riches. Simply saving money in a bank account lets your money lose value against inflation and prevents growth of your wealth. When you invest, though, you allow your money to work for you.

One of the most famous people in the media industry, Oprah Winfrey is aware of the need of wise investments. Oprah's road to riches was not only about her television job but also about her capacity to use her brand for successful ventures. She purchased a share in Harpo Productions in 1986, transforming it into among the most profitable production firms worldwide. Her idea of building riches was about owning it, not only about earning money, and carefully using her income to generate more.

Investing is for everyone who wants to systematically increase their money, not only for the wealthy or those with experience in finance. Early, even small investments made by you will eventually help you to create riches. Compound interest—where the rewards on your investments create more returns—will help you more the earlier you start.

One is 1. Recognizing Compounding's Power

Often referred to as the "eighth wonder of the world," compound interest is defined as the result of adding earned interest on an investment to the principal amount, therefore determining future interest based on the increased total. This produces a snowball effect over time whereby your returns quicken and exponential growth results.

One outstanding example of someone who knew how to increase her money over time is Spanx's creator, Sara Blakely. Blakely developed her concept from a $5,000 investment into a billion-dollar company. She not only concentrated on making money from Spanx but also reinvested her earnings to create her fortune by keeping long-term investments knowing how quickly her wealth could expand.

For instance, in the first year you would get $70 if you invest $1,000 at a 7% annual return. Your $1,070 will make interest in the second year, producing $74.90. The compounding power increases with increasing length of investment for your money.

The important lesson is to begin investing right now. If you are diligent and patient, even little amounts can add up really significantly.

2. Creating Money from Investments

You have many options for investing your money. Your objectives, risk tolerance, and timeframe will determine your appropriate investing plan. For ladies who are committed to accumulate wealth, let's dissect the most often occurring forms of investing.

Investments in Stock Markets

Although the stock market comes with risk, it provides among the best possible returns on investment. Stocks are ownership interests in businesses; so, when those businesses do well, their stocks also do.

Buying individual stocks allows you to invest straight in particular businesses. Still, since stock values are erratic, this calls more study and may be riskier.

Designed to follow a market index, such as the S&P 500, Index Funds and ETFs—Exchange-Traded Funds—are collections of stocks or bonds. Purchasing ETFs or index funds offers diversification, therefore lowering the risk of your investing portfolio.

Former PepsiCo CEO Indra Nooyi is a shining model of using assets to create wealth. PepsiCo concentrated on long-term sustainable development under her direction, and by means of calculated innovation investments, the business attained amazing success. Her emphasis on juggling risk and reward is a fundamental lesson in stock market wealth development.

Real Estate Investments

One tangible asset that can offer cash flow through rental income as well as appreciation—value growth—is real estate. For long-term wealth-building, many women discover real estate to be the perfect investment. Real estate provides various benefits whether your purchase is a holiday rental, business space, or house:

Appreciation: Property values rise with time, which would let you profitably sell them.

Investing in rental homes will allow you monthly rent payments to create passive income.

Real estate purchases include tax benefits including deductions on mortgage interest and depreciation.

One of the sharks on the TV show "Shark Tank," real estate entrepreneur Barbara Corcoran is a shining illustration of how wealth may be created via real estate investment. She transformed a $1,000 loan into an empire in real estate at hundreds of millions of dollars. Her experience demonstrates how much real estate can yield given the correct approach.

links

Bonds are loans you provide governments or businesses in return for interest payments. Though they offer lesser returns, they are usually less dangerous than stocks. Women who wish to preserve cash while keeping a consistent income source could find bonds to be a good choice.

Corporate bonds, issued by businesses, have more risk but higher interest rates.

Considered a fantastic choice for cautious investors, municipal bonds—issued by local governments—often tax-free and lower-risk.

Considered among the safest kind of bonds, government bonds are issued by federal governments.

Group Funds

From many investors, mutual funds aggregate funds to purchase a diversified portfolio of stocks, bonds, or other assets. Professionals oversee these money, thus they are a fantastic choice for those who want a hands-off attitude to investing. They offer diversity, therefore distributing risk.

Third: Making a Long-Term Financial Strategy

Creating wealth requires a strategy more than just investing. A well-considered financial plan will enable you to create goals, monitor your development, and keep on target. A financial plan consists of:

Budget: Track your expenses and revenue. Make sure you routinely save and invest a fraction of your salary.

Clearly state the definition of financial success for you. Are you hoping to retire early? By a given age, amass a certain level of wealth? Your financial selections will reflect your ambitions.

Eliminating high-interest debt is an absolutely vital first step toward building wealth. Once debt is paid off, more of your income is free for savings and investments.

Having three to six months of living expenses saved aside in an emergency fund is really vital. This offers both financial safety net and mental calm.

Verify your sufficient insurance level. This covers life insurance, health insurance, and—if relevant—disabled insurance.

Co-chair of the Bill & Melinda Gates Foundation Melinda Gates has long promoted women's empowerment and financial independence. She has pushed women to invest in their future as she knows the value of planning, saving, and budgeting. Her charitable activities also fit a more general plan for the distribution of wealth.

Making and following a financial plan will enable you to keep concentrated on your long-term objectives for increasing wealth.

4. Maintaining Wealth: Guarding What You Created

You have to guard your wealth once you have it. Preserving wealth is future planning, risk management, and asset protection. These are some essential tactics:

Make sure you have a will, trust, or estate plan in place to guarantee your wealth passes on in line with your intentions. Additionally helping to lower estate taxes is this.

Don't lay all of your eggs in one basket; diversify. To lower risk, divide your assets—stocks, bonds, real estate, etc.—among several classes.

Think on how you might guard your possessions from creditors, lawsuits, or other hazards. This can call for using insurance policies or building legal entities like limited liability organizations, or LLCs.

Apart from her musical career, Rihanna has developed a fashion and cosmetics empire using her brand Fenty, therefore enabling her to diversify her wealth and income. Strategically building several revenue sources, Rihanna has guaranteed that her fortune keeps increasing under protection.

As vital as money production is preservation of wealth. By acting to protect your money, you make sure it keeps expanding and offers your family and yourself financial stability.

Chapter 4 Review: Important Notes

Invest early and regularly to use compounding's ability to grow wealth.

To reduce risk, mix your assets—stocks, bonds, real estate, and other items.

Plan your finances including debt management, emergency savings, budgeting, and goal-setting.

Use asset protection techniques, diversification, and estate planning to guard your fortune.

What's Next?

The last stage in the wealth-building process—getting economic power—will be covered in Chapter 5. You will discover ways to maximize your money resources to influence your life, your neighborhood, and the surroundings more broadly.

yes

Good! Turning now to Chapter 5: Gaining Economic Power. This chapter will show you how to use your wealth to acquire not only financial independence but also economic power—the capacity to control your own destiny, influence others, and make significant decisions that can help to define your future. We will also feature inspirational stories of wealthy women who have made a lifetime of impact from their riches.

Chapter 5: Getting Economic Authority

Background:

Building wealth is not only about accumulating money. True wealth helps you to develop economic power, which goes beyond just financial independence. Economic power offers you the flexibility to make choices, the opportunity to design your destiny, and the capability to impact the world around you. In this chapter, we'll cover how you can move from financial security to economic empowerment—using your wealth as a tool to generate chances, build legacies, and leave a lasting influence.

One is 1. The Authority of Fiscal Independence

You are free from a job or the conventional 9–to- 5 when you reach financial independence. You are free to pursue your passions, make decisions for yourself, and mold your life on your own. The foundation of financial power is financial freedom.

Through her work at the Bill & Melinda Gates Foundation, Melinda Gates, for instance, epitribes this idea. She not only used her financial independence to donate globally but also used her platform to fight women's rights and economic empowerment—especially for women in underdeveloped nations. Using her riches and power, she has evolved into an advocate for change supporting programs targeted at gender equality, healthcare, and education.

Mastering the foundations of budgeting, investing, and asset creation will help one reach financial freedom. However, it also involves acting strategically to make sure your wealth keeps increasing while you are working for you so you may live life as it suits you.

Second: Creating Influence with Richness

The second phase is to utilize your wealth deliberately to acquire influence once you have the financial freedom to make decisions. Wealth allows you to change attitudes, influence decisions, and fight for causes dear to your heart.

Imagine Oprah Winfrey once more. Her media empire has helped her to influence public opinion and improve significant dialogues. She is a cultural influencer as well as a media powerhouse, able to raise awareness of topics close to her using her wealth and position. Whether it's supporting women's rights, healthy living, or education, Oprah's riches has enabled her to raise her voice in ways that have resonance all around.

Building influence is leveraging your resources to generate possibilities, open doors, and strengthen relationships that can enable you to advance your objectives. It's crucial to consider how best to strategically match your resources to your goal as you increase money.

2. The Function of Social Capital: Connections and Networking

Although your riches might give you tools, social capital—the relationships and connections you have—can greatly boost your impact. As you increase your riches, pay special attention to developing relationships that would help you voice your ideas and forward your objectives.

Former PepsiCo CEO Indra Nooyi models this approach. She frequently discusses how developing a strong network and developing contacts with influential politicians in politics and business has enabled her to take front stage in corporate America. Pushing for more diversity and inclusion in the corporate sector, she used her position and influence to create chances for women and minorities.

Good networking is about creating real connections, helping people, and figuring out cooperative projects for mutual benefit—not about going to fancy events or joining restricted circles. Remember to invest in your network as you create riches; it is among the most valuable tool you will have.

4. < Leveraging riches for social benefit

Using your fortune to change the world is one of the most liberating features of economic power. Wealth is about the possibility to leave a good impact on society, not only about luxury and enjoyment.

One really good illustration of this is Rihanna. She has sponsored healthcare projects, disaster assistance, and educational programs via her Clara Lionel Foundation, therefore leveraging her riches. Her emphasis on returning to underprivileged areas shows how riches may be a tool for transformation by means of financial resources profoundly affecting daily life.

Acquiring financial strength is about building systems that enable people to flourish, not about hoarding riches. You can gift more the more you build. Wealth can be a weapon for good social change whether your means of contribution are philanthropy, social enterprise investment, or personal initiative starting point.

3. Developing Legacies and Empowering Others

Real economic power is about enabling others and leaving a legacy that endures, not only about what you can accomplish personally. Mentoring others, sharing your experience, and providing financial assistance to rising leaders helps create a ripple effect that goes much beyond your own life.

Spanx's founder, Sara Blakely, epitribes this idea. Apart from developing her multi-billion dollar business, Blakely has made investments in empowering women via programs like the Sara Blakely Foundation, which concentrates on supporting women with education, entrepreneurship, and equipments required for success.

Whether through family wealth, business operations, or instruction of others on financial management, you can also leave a legacy by passing down information. By doing this, you start an empowering circle spanning decades.

06. Financial education as a means of economic empowerment

You have to learn about money if you want to acquire actual economic power. This is about knowing how to utilize money as a tool to influence, generate possibilities, and propel change—not only about how to save and invest.

Real estate powerhouse from Shark Tank, Barbara Corcoran, always stresses the need of financial literacy. Learning how to properly handle money and make wise financial decisions is, she thinks, one of the most important steps in reaching economic dominance. Barbara discovered how to use her financial acumen to create a fortune on her path from waitress to business magnate, and she has since committed herself to imparting that knowledge to others.

You will be more suited to use your riches for empowerment the more knowledge you have of money, investing, and financial markets. Financial literacy is power in the modern world; therefore, women should maximize that power in all spheres of their life.

Chapter 5 Review: Principal Learning Points

Getting economic power starts with reaching financial freedom.

Make calculated use of your riches to establish authority and raise your profile.

To increase your impact and open fresh opportunities, network and create social capital.

Use your riches to have a societal influence; avoid concentrating only on acquiring and instead concentrate on returning.

Empower others and transmit your body of knowledge to create a legacy.

A weapon for economic empowerment is financial education; engage in studying and expand your financial understanding.

What comes next?

Turning our attention to Personal Growth and Financial Wellness in the next chapter will explore the attitudes, behaviors, and daily routines that will enable you to keep a balanced existence while increasing your money.

Tell me how this sounds. All set to carry on or change anything?

4o diminutive

fine but add some unusual element.

stated:

Right! Allow this chapter to get some additional vitality and enthusiasm injected into it. We will concentrate on creating the material interesting, inspiring, and loaded with very relevant anecdotes. Here is a revised, somewhat more stylish Chapter 5: Gaining Economic Power:

Chapter 5: Getting Financial Authority

Introduction: The Authority Beyond Finance

Let's start with one clear point: although money is power, actual economic power? That is on a completely other level. Economic power goes beyond a huge bank account. It's about autonomy, power, and the capacity to help to choose your own future. Imagine living life on your terms: deciding what employment fascinates you, generating possibilities for others, and guiding choices impacting the planet. This chapter is all about how to move from being financially independent to becoming a real powerhouse of wealth—and how to use that power to design the life and legacy you desire.

One is The Freedom of Economic Independence

Your pass to a lifetime of choice is financial independence. That is the instant you understand you can live your life without asking permission from anyone. You can follow your interests, make audacious choices, and take measured chances. And believe me, this event will seem to be unique.

Speak about Melinda Gates. She stopped at being a billionaire through her marriage, not at one thing. Following her divorce, she rebuilt herself leading the Bill & Melinda Gates Foundation and emphasizing issues such global health, gender equality, and education. With her riches, she is not only enjoying her greatest life but also helping millions of others shape their futures. Financial freedom is the ability to do with money once you have it, not only about the money.

Your platform is financial independence to build, invent, and really live free. It's about filling your life with meaning, influence, and yes, even a little fun—not only about stuffing your pockets!

Two: Creating Influence with Wealth: You Are the Boss

As one accumulates wealth, what happens? You have influence. And the magic occurs here. In places where others would be caught on the sidelines, wealth allows you the capacity to move faster, talk louder, and create waves.

Imagine Oprah Winfrey. She created a platform that altered culture, not only a TV dynasty. Oprah inspired millions by using her riches to support causes and increase awareness. She used her influence to lead and to transform lives; she did not seek permission. She purposefully established her empire utilizing riches to support women's rights, education, and social justice.

We are discussing a type of influence here. Building your riches generates chances for others, not only improves your own life. You come to be someone people pay attention to, someone whose viewpoint counts. Whether you are addressing a tiny gathering of ardent supporters or a million-person audience, you are the ruler.

three. The secret weapon for power is networking.

Consider riches as a sort of magnifying lens. When you have it, your capacity for relationships gets much more potent. Wealth is about developing a network of incredible individuals who will enable you to reach your desired destination, not only about money.

See former PepsiCo CEO Indra Nooyi. She not only rose to become a worldwide leader but also deliberately fostered strong ties amongst several sectors. Nooyi developed relationships with other corporate executives, philanthropists, and inventors, so she did not reach the top working alone. These relationships enabled her to make major decisions and influence events on a worldwide basis.

Start considering the power of your network as you grow wealthy. You want to build relationships that will open doors, present fresh chances, and enable you to develop rather than only amassing money. Your weapon is your network. Use it to increase your voice and enable more forceful actions.

four. Wealth as a Social Change Agent

Having wealth allows you to make really transforming decisions about how you spend it. And when you consider how you might influence others instead of only your money account, you can have a significant global impact.

One very good example is Rihanna. Her riches enabled her to start the Clara Lionel Foundation, supporting projects in education, healthcare, and disaster relief rather than only enable her to make top-notch records. Rihanna used her position and money to transform underprivileged areas; she did not lounge in luxury.

Having economic power is about using that riches to improve the world rather than about only purchasing luxury goods or paying debts. There are countless opportunities. Wealth can be your vehicle for social change whether your financing is for job creation in underprivileged areas, women in business, or educational programs.

The fifth is Establishing a Legacy: Your Income, Your Influence

Let us now address something much beyond the here and now. We discuss legacy here. It's about leveraging riches to create something enduring, not only about amassing fortune. Starting to use your resources to empower others leaves left a legacy that surpasses you.

Consider Sara Blakely, the Spanx founder. Her path was not only in creating a billion-dollar company but also in enabling women to seize their life. By means of her Sara Blakely Foundation, she not only emphasizes returning but also supports women aspiring to success. She is guiding people toward their own glass ceilings broken.

Creating a legacy means you are determining the course of events for next generations. Your influence will be felt long after you're gone whether it's passing on riches, knowledge, or enabling others to occupy your place in the world.

six. Financial Education: Your most valuable tool is knowledge.

The road to economic power is about knowing what to do with what you acquire, not only about earning. Regarding money, investments, and financial plan, you have to learn. Knowledge is more than just power; it's economic power.

Real estate whiz and Shark Tank investor Barbara Corcoran understands the value of financial literacy. She began with very little, but by learning about the business, making wise investments, and grabbing possibilities she built her real estate empire. Her pass to power was financial knowledge.

How therefore may one become financially literate? First, pick up the foundations of financial markets, budgeting, and investing. Study books, go to seminars, and consult professionals. You will be more suited to convert your wealth into actual, long-lasting financial power the more knowledge you possess.

Chapter 5 Review: Principal Learning Points

Being financially independent lets you design the life you want.

Richness is about the impact you have to change the world, not only about what you can buy.

Create a strong network that enable you to ascend higher and find voice.

Whether by social effect, investments, or philanthropy, use your riches to change things.

Empower others and forward your knowledge and tools to create a legacy.

Your most effective tool is financial education; apply it to increase your economic power.

What comes next?

We shall explore Personal Growth and Financial Wellness in the next chapter—the attitudes and everyday practices that will keep you strong and balanced while you travel toward prosperity.

Tell me how this rendition performs for you. If you would want, I may change or add anything to increase its appeal.

Saying:

forthcoming chapter

Definitely! Let us build on the enthusiasm and explore Chapter 6: Personal Development and Financial Wellness. Emphasizing the habits, attitudes, and everyday activities that will enable you to keep on track as you increase your wealth, this chapter will concentrate on the relationship between personal development and financial well-being.

Chapter Six: Financial Wellness and Personal Development

Introduction: Internal Work of Wealth

Many times, we consider money as a physical asset—that which we can hold, spend, or invest. Actually, though, real riches comes from inside. You must first concentrate on developing a mindset and personal behaviors that will keep you grounded, disciplined, and in line with your goals before you can create external wealth. Financial health is about your relationship with money and how you prioritize your well-being while negotiating the path of wealth-building, not only about your income.

This chapter will show how vital to attaining long-term financial success are creating personal growth habits including mindset changes, everyday activities, and self-care practices. Let's discuss the inner work needed to create not only your financial wellbeing but also your personal power and prosperity.

The first is The Mindset Shift: Abundance Over Scarcity

To unleash financial freedom, you need to change from a mindset of scarcity to one of plenty. Scarcity thinking teaches you you have to battle for your position in the world since resources are few and there is not enough to go around. Many often, this kind of thinking keeps people caught in a cycle of anxiety and lack—afraid to try new activities, take chances, or make personal investments.

But everything changes when you start to live from wealth. You start to notice chances instead of challenges. You realize that wealth, success, and opportunity abound; moreover, the more you offer, the more you draw.

Think about Oprah Winfrey, for instance. She has talked about how her success has been mostly dependent on a plentiful attitude and thanks. Oprah generated opportunities by changing her perspective on the world, not merely waited for them to arrive. She felt that there was always more, and this abundance drove her development and achievement.

First change your language to welcome plenty. Saying, "How can I afford that?" instead of, "I can't afford that," can help you to see opportunities and support your conviction that riches is not only realistic but also unavoidable.

Two: Daily Habits: Results Equate to Consistency

One cannot achieve financial success over night. It is developed over time by consistent behavior. Those that show up daily are the most successful people; they are not always the smartest or most gifted. They establish daily routines fit for their objectives, and these little deeds add up over time to produce enormous effects.

One striking illustration is Marie Forleo, the author of Everything is Figureoutable and businesswoman. Marie's achievement resulted from years of consistent behavior rather than from one major choice. Her daily routines of showing up for her community, producing worthwhile material, and developing her abilities helped her to build her company. These little behaviors accumulated over time to produce a profitable multi-million dollar brand.

Ask yourself as you accumulate wealth: What behaviors can enable me to approach my financial objectives? Little, deliberate acts add up whether it's reading 10 pages of a finance book every day, checking your money monthly, or spending 15 minutes each morning to plan your daily activities.

Thirdly Time Management: Learning to Balance

Managing your personal life with your financial goals is one of the main difficulties of wealth-building. The grind may easily enthralls one and cause one to feel as though one must labor nonstop to realize their aspirations. That kind of thinking, though, can cause burnout and jeopardize your health.

Developing the capacity to prioritize your time will help you to really achieve financial wellbeing. Time is your most valuable resource; once it runs out, you cannot get it back.

After a personal health crisis, Arianna Huffington, creator of The Huffington Post and Thrive author, started advocating wellness and work-life balance. She came to see that success without wellness wasn't really success and that she had been overburdling herself. She now promotes, along with the hustle, giving sleep, self-care, and mindfulness top priority.

Learning to balance job with family, self-care, and personal development requires mastery of time management. It's about establishing limits and planning to free you to concentrate on what really matters. Make good use of your time; keep in mind that it is more important on how efficiently you use it than on your work quantity.

Four. Success's Foundation: Self-Care and Well-Being

The adage "You can't pour from an empty cup" is true: building money calls for a clean mind, keen attention, and emotional resilience—all of which are absent if you neglect yourself.

Founder of Girls Who Code Reshma Saujani discusses throughout her path to success the need of mental health and self-compassion. She understands that, in creating her enterprise, breaks, meditation, and physical activity were just as important as her business plans.

Whether your self-care consists in walking, meditating, journaling, or just spending time with loved ones, include it into your schedule. These techniques can help you get the insight you need to make the greatest decisions for your money and future, as well as reenergize you and lessen stress.

5. Emotional health meets money management in financial wellness.

Financial wellness addresses your emotional connection with money rather than only your bank account. Whether it's spending, saving, or investing, women too frequently feel guilty or stressed about money. This emotional baggage can prevent you from confidently generating wealth and from making empowered financial decisions.

TV personality and financial expert Suze Orman guides women toward empowerment from knowledge and self-worth. When you view money as a tool for security, freedom, and impact instead of something to worry about, you can start to make decisions with a clear, cool head.

Start building financial wellness by looking at your feelings about money. Do you find it threatening? Do you view it as a necessary evil, or do you welcome it as a tool for improving the life you live or that of others? Changing your emotional relationship to money can help you to start wise and confidently managing it.

Chapter 6 Review: salient Features

Mindset is essential; move from scarcity to abundance and chances will abound.

Consistency is important; little everyday activities taken over time add up to great effects.

Time management is a balancing act; design a calendar fit for your personal well-being and financial objectives.

Self-care is fundamental; take care of your body, mind, and emotions to enable you to present totally for your path of wealth-building.

Understanding your emotional connection with money will help you to take charge of it and build a better financial future.

What comes next?

The following chapter will explore money and Legacy—how to not only build money but also preserve and forward it to succeeding generations. Your path to financial freedom shapes the life of those you love for years to come, so it goes much beyond you.

Four o mini

yes

Amazing! Let's carry on with Chapter 7: Wealth and Legacy, which addresses how to create not just riches but also a legacy that will help next generations as well as you. This chapter will go over generational wealth, the need of building financial security for your family, and how you could use your riches to have a good influence.

Chapter 7: Wealth and Legacy

Introduction: Apart from the Bank Account

Creating riches is a great and transforming trip. True wealth, however, is about leaving a legacy that will carry your values, purpose, and vision forward for next generations, not only about amassing assets and savings. It's about realizing that the wealth you build and the money you make may be the basis for others so they may flourish, follow their aspirations, and start generational cycles free from poverty.

This chapter will look at the value of leaving a legacy, how to preserve your wealth for next generations, and how to maximize your financial influence. The objective is to turn your attention from just accumulating riches to leaving a strong, enduring legacy that benefits not only your family but also your community, causes you care about, and the earth at large.

One can find: defining legacy: wealth transcends money.

When we consider legacy, most of us consider money or assets—land, property, investments. Although those are crucial components of leaving a financial legacy, they are only a minor puzzle piece. Whether it is your principles, beliefs, or the good change you brought about in the world, true legacy is about what you pass on.

consider Maya Angelou, for instance. Maya left a legacy of empowerment and resiliency, not only books of poetry and storytelling. Generations of people have been motivated by her teachings to welcome their inner power, fight for their worth, and carry others along the road. Maya Angelou left behind not only her writings but also a mindset of empowerment, tenacity, and love.

Within the framework of wealth, your legacy consists in more than simply financial resources; it also consists in the wisdom and tools required to increase wealth, live with purpose, and reach personal fulfillment. This will enable your loved ones—just as you have done—to establish their own legacies.

In 2. Creating Generation Wealth: A Long Term Plan

A notion that has proved essential in producing long-lasting success for companies, communities, and families is generational wealth. But it's about making strategic, deliberate decisions that maintain and increase wealth across several generations, not only about passing on assets. The plan is to provide next generations with the skills, knowledge, and financial literacy required to maintain and expand upon the riches you have produced.

Once more, Oprah Winfrey presents a really outstanding model. Oprah is more concerned in building chances for others—including her family and her team—than in her own needs. Oprah has established a platform for riches and success that will keep expanding so her family members may start their own companies, have their own influence, and preserve the financial independence she has so laboriously developed.

You have to be long-term thinking if you want generational riches. This indicates:

Making good financial decisions that will appreciate over time—stocks, real estate, etc.—and investing sensibly

Teaching financial literacy to your children, nieces, nephews, and anybody else you may positively impact will help them to grasp money's workings and how to create wealth for themselves.

Establishing trusts, investments, and estate plans that protect your fortune long after you're gone.

three. Conserving Your Legacy: Approaches for Maintenance

Making wealth is simply one aspect; the other is ensuring that it will be safeguarded for next generations. Without appropriate protection plans, taxes, bad investments, or even family conflicts can all help to diminish wealth.

Making a trust or estate plan will help you to protect your riches most successfully. This guarantees tax-efficient passing on of your money to the appropriate persons. To guarantee that your fortune remains intact for the future generation, you must have a will, arrange life insurance, and engage with a financial advisor.

Co-chair of the Bill & Melinda Gates Foundation Melinda Gates is a shining illustration of legacy preservation and generosity. She has dedicated herself to preserving the riches her family has accumulated by making sure they are applied for humanitarian purposes, therefore fostering a legacy of social impact. The Gates family has built a foundation aiming at public health, poverty reduction, and worldwide fairness.

Including philanthropy into your legacy planning not only safeguards your fortune but also creates a legacy that will benefit others apart from your immediate family.

In 4. Returning Wealth as a Change Agent

Think about how you might use your riches as a tool for good while you amassing it. When utilized deliberately, wealth can be a great tool for bettering the lot of those in need, uplifting local communities, and addressing world problems.

Another outstanding example of giving back is Rihanna, who transformed her musical career into a multi-million dollar commercial empire. Particularly in underprivileged areas, Rihanna has concentrated on education, health, and disaster response projects using her Clara Lionel Foundation. Her business sense is as keen as her will to change the world.

Whether through philanthropy, social enterprise investment, or just running your company to help issues close to your heart, your legacy should naturally include giving back. It's about using your riches to change the world so that your success guarantees a better future for others rather than only benefits you.

5. Financial Independence: Equipping Your Kids to Excel

The gift of financial freedom is among the best ones you could present to any young person in your life or your own children. Leave them assets; also, teach them how to handle and increase their fortune. Make sure kids appreciate budgeting, saving, investing, and giving.

Look at Jessica Jackley, co-founder of Kiva, a nonprofit enabling individuals to provide microloans to business owners in underdeveloped nations Beginning early in her career, she has been concentrated in teaching financial literacy. She thinks that by teaching younger generations financial empowerment, you enable them to design their own wealth-building plans and help to break poverty cycles.

One does not need children to pass on this insight. Guideline others. Tell us about your financial management experiences and lessons discovered. This guarantees not only that your legacy lives but also that you enable others to follow in your footsteps.

Chapter 7 Review: salient features

Legacy is about the ideals, ideas, and influence you leave behind—not about money.

Generational wealth requires intentional action, smart investing, and teaching financial literacy.

Protect your wealth through estate planning, trusts, and other financial strategies.

Give back—use your wealth to create positive change and leave a legacy of philanthropy.

Teach future generations the tools to manage, grow, and invest their wealth for themselves.

What's Next:

In the next chapter, we'll delve into Mindful Wealth-Building—how to align your money with your values and purpose, so that every dollar you earn and invest feels fulfilling. You'll learn how to create a path to wealth that's both financially successful and personally rewarding.

Great! Let's move on to Chapter 8: Mindful Wealth-Building, where we explore the alignment of your financial goals with your core values. In this chapter, we will discuss how to create a wealth-building strategy that not only achieves financial success but also feels fulfilling and aligned with your purpose. This chapter will help you recognize that wealth is not just about money—it's about living a life of intention and impact.

Chapter 8: Mindful Wealth-Building

Introduction: Aligning Wealth with Purpose

In a world where financial success is often measured by how much you have, it's easy to forget that wealth is more than just a number in a bank account. True wealth is about living a life that is aligned with your values and purpose—a life where your money is not only working for you, but also for the causes, people, and goals that matter most to you.

This chapter will explore how to build wealth with mindfulness, ensuring that every step you take in your wealth-building journey feels aligned with your personal values and brings you a sense of fulfillment. It's about making conscious financial decisions, whether it's your spending, saving, or investing, that reflect the kind of life you want to live and the legacy you want to leave.

1. The Power of Mindful Money Decisions

We often make financial decisions based on external influences—what society expects, what our friends are doing, or even what the media tells us we should want. But, true financial freedom and success come from making mindful decisions that are deeply rooted in your values and long-term goals.

Mindful money decisions involve being present in the moment and intentionally choosing how to spend, save, and invest based on what truly matters to you. Serena Williams, a world-renowned athlete and entrepreneur, exemplifies this mindset in her financial and business endeavors. She has built a significant fortune, not only through her career but also by creating brands that reflect her personal values of empowerment and equality.

Mindful wealth-building isn't just about achieving financial success—it's about ensuring that the way you accumulate and spend wealth aligns with your deeper purpose. It's about taking responsibility for your financial life and making decisions that honor both your personal and professional growth.

2. Financial Freedom Through Purposeful Earning

Earning money should not feel like a burden or a constant chase. It should feel like an extension of who you are—a reflection of your skills, passions, and purpose. When your work aligns with your personal values, the act of earning becomes empowering and fulfilling.

Beyoncé is a perfect example of someone who has built financial freedom through a purposeful career. She's not only a global music icon, but she's also built a business empire that promotes creativity, diversity, and social change. Beyoncé's success isn't just about the money—it's about having a platform to make an impact in the world, create change, and build a legacy for herself and her family.

To build mindful wealth, it's important to find meaning in your work and ensure that your career or business reflects your passions. If you feel aligned with the work you do, money becomes a natural byproduct of your effort, rather than something you constantly need to chase.

3. Investing with Intention: Aligning Your Portfolio with Your Values

Investing is a powerful tool for wealth-building, but it's important to invest with intention. You can grow your wealth while staying true to your values by choosing investments that reflect the causes you care about. This means considering impact investing, socially responsible investing, or green funds—where your money works for both your financial future and the planet's future.

Emma Watson, actress and activist, is a prime example of someone who uses her wealth to fund initiatives that reflect her values. She has been an advocate for gender equality and sustainable fashion, investing in companies that prioritize environmental sustainability and ethical production.

By aligning your investments with your values, you not only build wealth but also contribute to causes that matter to you. You can choose investments that impact communities, promote social justice, or support environmental sustainability—helping you build a portfolio that reflects your commitment to a better future.

4. Creating a Mindful Budget: Aligning Spending with Values

Your spending habits play a key role in how your wealth reflects your personal values. A mindful budget involves not only tracking your expenses but also consciously choosing where your money goes. It's about evaluating your purchases and ensuring that your money is being spent on things that truly support your well-being, happiness, and long-term goals.

Take Michelle Obama as an example. She has always been intentional about how she spends her money, whether it's supporting healthy eating initiatives, promoting education, or investing in causes that empower women. Michelle's spending decisions reflect her commitment to health, education, and empowerment—values that guide her actions both personally and professionally.

To create a mindful budget, ask yourself: Does this spending decision align with my values? Will this purchase help me grow personally, professionally, or financially? If not, consider shifting your spending to reflect your true desires and goals.

5. Living Your Values in All Areas of Life

Mindful wealth-building extends beyond finances. It involves aligning your entire life with your values and purpose. Your time, energy, and relationships are just as important as your money. If you spend your time and energy on things that don't align with your values, you'll find yourself feeling drained and disconnected from your true purpose.

Sheryl Sandberg, COO of Facebook and author of Lean In, is an excellent example of someone who lives her values both in her professional and personal life. She advocates for women's empowerment, gender equality, and the importance of work-life balance. Sheryl ensures that her life is aligned with her mission to create more opportunities for women in leadership, and this alignment is reflected in the work she does and the companies she supports.

Living your values means making intentional decisions in all areas of life—not just finances. Whether it's how you spend your free time, the relationships you nurture, or the work you take on, ensuring everything is aligned with your purpose brings a sense of fulfillment and peace.

Chapter 8 Recap: Key Takeaways

Mindful money decisions are rooted in your values, ensuring that every financial choice you make brings you closer to your purpose.

Purposeful earning is about aligning your career or business with your passions, allowing financial success to flow naturally.

Investing with intention means choosing investments that reflect the causes and values you care about, such as impact investing or sustainable funds.

Mindful budgeting involves spending with intention—ensuring that your purchases align with your long-term goals and values.

Living a life aligned with your values means being intentional with your time, energy, and relationships, leading to deeper fulfillment.

What's Next:

In the next chapter, we'll explore the final step in your journey to financial success: Sustaining Wealth for the Long Haul. We'll discuss how to ensure that the wealth you've built remains secure and continues to grow over time, even when faced with challenges or unexpected changes.

Awesome! Let's move on to Chapter 9: Sustaining Wealth for the Long Haul, where we dive into the strategies and mindset needed to ensure the wealth you've built continues to grow and thrive throughout your life. We'll talk about how to manage your wealth over time, prepare for financial setbacks, and pass on your legacy.

Chapter 9: Sustaining Wealth for the Long Haul

Introduction: Building Wealth for Today and Tomorrow

Building wealth is one thing. But maintaining and growing it over the long term is a whole different ball game. True financial success isn't just about getting rich; it's about staying rich and ensuring your wealth continues to work for you and future generations. In this chapter, we'll explore how to create systems, habits, and strategies that will keep your wealth flowing—no matter what life throws your way.

Sustaining wealth requires a forward-thinking mindset that includes smart financial planning, risk management, and a deep understanding of long-term goals. It's about creating a strong financial foundation that stands the test of time.

1. Wealth as a Long-Term Mindset

Wealth isn't just a sprint to the finish line; it's a marathon. One of the most important things you can do as you build your wealth is to develop a long-term mindset. This means thinking beyond the immediate gratification of today and considering how your decisions today will impact your financial future.

Consider Oprah Winfrey, one of the most influential women in the world. Oprah's rise to success wasn't an overnight phenomenon. She's built her empire over decades, consistently making decisions with an eye on the long term. Oprah's wealth didn't come just from her talk show; it came from strategic investments, business ventures, and a long-term vision for her career. Oprah didn't just want to be wealthy today—she wanted to build a legacy that would last long after she left the screen.

To sustain your wealth, you must think of it as a long-term project. Focus on the bigger picture, rather than immediate rewards, and be patient in your journey. This mindset helps you stay disciplined, avoid impulsive decisions, and make strategic choices that serve you in the long run.

2. Creating a Legacy of Wealth: Passing the Torch

One of the most powerful ways to sustain wealth is by thinking about your legacy. Wealth-building isn't just for you; it can also be about securing the financial future for your family, your community, and the causes you care about. By passing on knowledge, assets, and values to the next generation, you create a lasting legacy of financial empowerment.

Rihanna has not only built a career worth billions but also created a lasting legacy through her brand, investments, and philanthropy. She is actively working to build a foundation of economic independence for young women through her ventures, proving that wealth can extend beyond personal enrichment. By creating businesses like Fenty Beauty, which empowers women of all skin tones, and focusing on giving back to communities, Rihanna is ensuring that her wealth serves a broader purpose for years to come.

To build a legacy, start thinking about how you can teach financial literacy to those around you, create trusts and wills that ensure your wealth is distributed according to your wishes, and support causes that align with your values. Your legacy isn't just about passing down assets—it's about creating a mindset of financial freedom that will live on.

3. Managing Risk: Protecting Your Wealth from Setbacks

The journey to wealth isn't always a smooth ride. There will be ups and downs, and the key to sustaining wealth is knowing how to protect it from unexpected setbacks, such as economic downturns, market crashes, or personal financial crises.

To manage risk effectively, ensure that you have a diversified portfolio of investments and multiple income streams. You want to build a buffer to weather the storms that may come. Having a mix of stocks, real estate, bonds, and even alternative investments (like art or cryptocurrency) can provide protection from market fluctuations.

Sheryl Sandberg also embodies the principle of risk management. After the unexpected loss of her husband, Sheryl had to navigate both emotional and financial upheaval. Her resilience is a testament to the importance of having multiple streams of income, saving for rainy days, and investing wisely. By creating a financial cushion and maintaining a diverse portfolio, Sheryl was able to safeguard her wealth, even in the most challenging times.

Incorporating insurance (health, life, disability) and creating an emergency fund should also be part of your wealth-sustaining plan. These measures will allow you to weather financial storms without losing your progress.

4. Building Smart Systems: Automating Your Wealth Growth

One of the smartest ways to ensure your wealth continues to grow over time is by creating systems that automatically put your money to work. Automation is a powerful tool in financial planning. Whether it's setting up automatic contributions to retirement accounts, investment portfolios, or savings funds, the less you have to think about your money, the more you can focus on growing it.

Melinda Gates, co-chair of the Bill & Melinda Gates Foundation, uses her platform to advocate for women's health, education, and empowerment. But behind her wealth, she has also built systems of giving back, ensuring that her resources continue to grow while also benefiting global causes. She's an advocate for financial inclusion and encourages women to automate their financial habits for future growth and security.

By setting up automatic savings, recurring investments, and ensuring that you're consistently contributing to your financial future, you can build wealth that grows without requiring constant effort. Let the system work for you, while you work on creating more opportunities for your wealth to grow.

5. Staying Educated: The Power of Lifelong Learning

Sustaining wealth isn't just about protecting it—it's also about continuously growing it. One of the best ways to do this is by staying educated on financial trends, market changes, and new investment opportunities. Lifelong learning is key to ensuring that your wealth remains relevant and continues to increase in value over time.

Martha Stewart, a self-made businesswoman, continually evolves her business empire. She has leveraged her knowledge of home décor, cooking, and lifestyle to expand her brand, keeping up with changing consumer tastes. By continuously learning and innovating, Martha has kept her wealth-building strategies fresh and relevant in an ever-changing world.

Invest in your financial education by reading, attending workshops, and staying updated on industry trends. Financial literacy isn't a one-time achievement—it's a continuous process that keeps you prepared to make informed decisions as your wealth grows.

Chapter 9 Recap: Key Takeaways

Building wealth is a long-term mindset, focused on patience, discipline, and strategic decision-making.

Creating a legacy of wealth involves thinking about the impact you want to leave and ensuring your wealth benefits future generations.

Risk management is essential—diversify your investments, create an emergency fund, and protect your wealth with insurance.

Automation helps you save time and energy while your wealth grows on autopilot—automate your savings, investments, and retirement contributions.

Lifelong learning keeps your financial strategies fresh and adaptable, ensuring that your wealth remains strong over time.

What's Next:

In the final chapter, we'll explore how to celebrate your success and continue to evolve your financial journey. It's time to embrace the wealth you've built, enjoy the fruits of your labor, and keep growing in your financial power.

make it more interesting

Sure! Let's add some more energy, storytelling, and actionable insights to make the chapter more engaging and captivating.

Chapter 9: Sustaining Wealth for the Long Haul

Introduction: Wealth Isn't a Sprint, It's a Marathon

We've discussed how to earn wealth, but what about keeping it? Building wealth is thrilling, but sustaining it over time is where the true magic happens. It's about playing the long game—making decisions today that ensure your financial future is just as bright as your present. In this chapter, we'll uncover how to nurture and protect your wealth in a way that will serve you, your family, and your legacy for decades to come.

Sustaining wealth is a different skillset altogether. It requires a strategic mindset, savvy decisions, and the willingness to evolve. The road ahead might be full of twists and turns, but with the right tools, you can make sure that your wealth isn't a fleeting moment—it's a sustainable empire.

1. Long-Term Thinking: Building Wealth That Lasts

Let's be honest—instant wealth is seductive. Quick wins, shiny cars, lavish vacations—who wouldn't want that? But when the allure of the fast track fades, what you're left with is a lasting legacy built on slow and steady wins the race.

Take a page out of Oprah Winfrey's playbook. From humble beginnings to billionaire mogul, Oprah's rise was no accident. She wasn't just building her empire for today—she was thinking decades ahead. Every move she made, every business venture she took on, was with an eye on longevity. She didn't just want success—she wanted a legacy of empowerment that would outlive her. Today, her wealth continues to grow through investments like Fenty Beauty, her own production company, and various philanthropic ventures that keep giving back.

The key to long-term wealth is thinking beyond the next paycheck. When you build wealth, think of it as planting seeds that will blossom over time. Imagine a garden that you'll tend to with care, and one day, it will bear fruit that feeds generations.

2. Creating a Legacy: Building Wealth That Transcends You

You're not just building wealth for today—you're building it for tomorrow, and the next generation after that. The legacy you create today can change the course of future generations.

Rihanna has not only turned her music career into a global empire but has strategically expanded her brand into Fenty Beauty, which was designed to cater to all women, regardless of skin tone. Rihanna's wealth doesn't just benefit her; it has created opportunities for women of all backgrounds, giving them access to products and jobs they never had before. She's a trailblazer, showing that wealth can have a far-reaching social impact.

When you think about your own wealth-building journey, consider how you can pass down more than money. Teach financial literacy, create a family trust, and leave guidelines for future generations on how to keep growing the wealth you've built. Don't just leave assets behind—leave behind a blueprint for success.

3. Managing Risk: Staying Resilient When the Market Shakes

The road to financial freedom isn't always smooth. In fact, there will be bumps, potholes, and maybe even a few steep hills. But how you handle risk is one of the most important aspects of sustaining your wealth.

Enter Sheryl Sandberg, who faced unimaginable personal tragedy with the sudden death of her husband. Yet, her ability to bounce back, financially and emotionally, was a testament to her resilience. Sheryl had already built her wealth by investing in Facebook and creating Lean In—but it was her focus on diversified investments and the steps she took to ensure her financial security that helped her through tough times.

To weather financial storms, make sure your wealth is well-diversified. Think beyond stocks—consider real estate, business ventures, and even alternative assets like cryptocurrency or fine art. Also, keep an emergency fund on hand, and don't neglect insurance. The goal is to have a financial cushion so that if the unexpected happens, your wealth remains untouched.

4. The Magic of Automation: Letting Your Money Work for You

There's a powerful concept that successful women know: automation is your best friend. Once you've set up a system, your wealth can grow in the background while you focus on what you do best.

Take Melinda Gates, for example. She didn't just build wealth for herself; she built a system of wealth that benefits women and children worldwide through the Bill & Melinda Gates

Foundation. While she was active in philanthropy, she used automation to build systems that allowed her wealth to grow steadily.

Setting up automatic savings, investments, and even contributions to retirement accounts is a game-changer. By automating your financial goals, you're taking the emotion out of it. You're ensuring that your wealth continues to grow, even when you're busy with life's other priorities.

5. The Power of Education: Never Stop Evolving

Wealth is not static. The financial landscape is constantly shifting, and if you want your wealth to evolve with it, education is key. Never stop learning, whether it's about new investment opportunities, financial trends, or personal growth.

Martha Stewart is a perfect example. From cookbooks to home goods to media mogul, she reinvented herself and her brand time and time again. What keeps her relevant, even decades into her career, is her ability to adapt and evolve. She continuously invests in herself, reading up on new trends, attending business seminars, and staying ahead of the curve.

Make it a point to read, attend workshops, and immerse yourself in learning about financial trends. As the world shifts, your ability to stay financially sharp will ensure that your wealth doesn't just stay in place—it grows.

Chapter 9 Recap: Key Takeaways

Long-term thinking: Building wealth isn't about quick wins. Think of your wealth-building as planting a garden—it takes time, care, and patience.

Create a legacy: Pass down knowledge, values, and assets to future generations. Don't just leave money—leave a blueprint for success.

Manage risk: Diversify your wealth, protect it with insurance, and have a strong emergency fund. Be resilient when the unexpected happens.

Automate your wealth: Set up systems that let your money grow without your constant involvement. Automate savings and investments.

Never stop learning: Educate yourself about financial opportunities, market changes, and strategies for wealth-building. Evolving is the key to staying relevant.

Next Steps:

In the final chapter, we'll shift gears to focus on how to celebrate your success and enjoy the fruits of your labor while continuing to grow. It's time to embrace your wealth, savor the journey, and look ahead to what's next.

Great! Let's make the chapter even more engaging and powerful. Here's the final refined version of Chapter 9, "Sustaining Wealth for the Long Haul", with even more emphasis on storytelling, actionability, and inspiration:

Chapter 9: Sustaining Wealth for the Long Haul

Introduction: Wealth Isn't a Sprint, It's a Marathon

In the whirlwind of building wealth, we often forget that the true test of financial success isn't just how much you accumulate—it's how long you can sustain it. Building wealth is thrilling, but preserving it for the long haul is where true financial mastery lies. It's about making decisions today that ensure your future wealth isn't just a fleeting moment but a lasting legacy.

Wealth isn't something you build in a day. It's a slow, careful journey—one that requires foresight, wisdom, and a strategic approach. If you want to see your wealth grow, evolve, and impact your life for years to come, you need to master the art of sustaining it.

1. Long-Term Thinking: Building Wealth That Lasts

Instant wealth can be intoxicating—quick wins, new opportunities, and a glamorous lifestyle. But the real test comes when the hustle slows down and the novelty wears off. What then?

Take Oprah Winfrey as an example. From her roots in rural Mississippi, Oprah didn't just build an empire to be enjoyed in the present. She built a multifaceted brand that would stand the test of time. Her investments in OWN, Fenty Beauty, and Apple TV+ weren't just about earning more; they were about legacy. She thought in decades, not years. Her wealth wasn't just made to be spent—it was made to empower, to create opportunities, and to keep growing.

What can you learn from Oprah's playbook? The answer is simple: Think long-term. Don't just chase the next paycheck. Build assets that will appreciate over time—invest in real estate, stocks, and business ventures that will continue to produce value for years, even when you're not actively working.

2. Creating a Legacy: Building Wealth That Transcends You

Wealth isn't just about how much you can spend in this lifetime. It's about how much impact you can make and how much you can pass on. It's about creating a legacy that will continue to shape the world long after you're gone.

Take Rihanna—her journey from a pop icon to a business mogul is inspiring, but what's even more impressive is how she's turning her wealth into a force for good. With Fenty Beauty, she disrupted the cosmetics industry, making it inclusive for every woman, no matter her skin tone. Rihanna didn't just create a brand; she created a movement, one that will endure far beyond her music career. Her wealth isn't about buying luxury items—it's about giving back and empowering others.

You can create a legacy too. Think beyond your immediate needs. Start by teaching the next generation about financial literacy, create family trusts, and plan how your wealth can continue to grow and support causes that matter to you. Leave behind more than assets— leave a blueprint for future success.

3. Managing Risk: Staying Resilient When the Market Shakes

The path to lasting wealth is rarely a straight line. There will be inevitable bumps in the road, market crashes, unexpected crises, and moments when everything seems uncertain. But how you respond to these challenges determines whether your wealth survives.

Sheryl Sandberg knows a thing or two about resilience. After losing her husband suddenly, she was faced with unimaginable grief and financial decisions that could have derailed her. Instead, she leaned on the very principles that made her a Silicon Valley powerhouse—diversification and strong financial planning.

To weather life's storms, you need a diversified portfolio. Don't put all your eggs in one basket. Spread your wealth across different asset classes—stocks, bonds, real estate, and even alternative investments like cryptocurrency or fine art. You also need a robust emergency fund, insurance, and a solid plan to pivot when times get tough. This way, when the market or life hits you hard, your wealth won't crumble—it will bounce back stronger.

4. The Magic of Automation: Letting Your Money Work for You

The more wealth you build, the more essential it becomes to automate your financial growth. Automation takes the stress out of wealth management and allows you to scale your success without constant intervention.

Look at Melinda Gates. She's not just a philanthropist—she's also an incredibly strategic investor. From Microsoft to her work at the Bill & Melinda Gates Foundation, Melinda automated many aspects of her wealth-building process. She used tools like automated investments, savings programs, and financial advisors to ensure her wealth would continue to grow, even when she was busy shaping global policy.

Set up automatic systems for your investments, savings, and even retirement. Let technology do the heavy lifting, so you can focus on what really matters: growing your empire, helping others, and living life on your terms.

5. The Power of Education: Never Stop Evolving

Wealth is ever-changing. The markets evolve, technology shifts, and new opportunities emerge every day. If you want your wealth to keep growing, you need to continuously learn and adapt.

Look at Martha Stewart, for example. She didn't just stop at being a TV personality or a lifestyle brand mogul—she's continually reinvented herself. She's launched new businesses, pivoted to digital platforms, and expanded her brand into new arenas. Her ability to evolve and adapt to changes in the marketplace is one of the reasons she's remained a household name.

The key to sustaining your wealth is education. Stay curious, keep learning, and invest in financial literacy. The more you know about the financial landscape, the better equipped you'll be to make decisions that keep your wealth growing. Attend workshops, read books, and engage with other powerful women to keep evolving in the world of finance.

Chapter 9 Recap: Key Takeaways

Long-term thinking: Build wealth with a vision that spans decades, not just years. Think of wealth-building as planting seeds for the future.

Create a legacy: Start planning today for a legacy that will impact future generations. Teach financial literacy, create family trusts, and make sure your wealth keeps growing.

Manage risk: Diversify your portfolio, have an emergency fund, and be resilient when unexpected challenges arise.

Automate your wealth: Use automation to grow your wealth without constant oversight. Set up systems that work for you.

Never stop learning: Education is key to evolving and adapting to changing financial landscapes. Keep learning about new financial opportunities, markets, and trends.

Next Steps:

In the next chapter, we'll shift gears and dive into how to celebrate your success while ensuring that you're always ready for the next chapter. Embrace your financial achievements, savor the journey, and get ready to set new goals.

yes

I'm glad you liked it! If you're ready to move forward with the next chapter or need any additional content, feel free to let me know. We can continue refining or adding new material as you go!

additional content

To add additional content and further enrich the book, here are some extra sections that can be woven in, either as bonus material or as added depth within the existing chapters:

Bonus Chapter: "The Wealth of Self-Care: Prioritizing Your Mental and Physical Health for Financial Success"

Introduction: Wealth Starts Within

While we often focus on the external process of building wealth—investing, saving, earning—one critical element gets overlooked: your mental and physical well-being. True wealth isn't just about money. It's about the holistic balance that allows you to perform at your best, day after day. This chapter emphasizes the importance of self-care as a cornerstone of long-term wealth.

1. The Relationship Between Mental Health and Financial Success

Have you ever felt overwhelmed by the pressures of growing your wealth, only to realize that stress and anxiety are interfering with your decision-making? This is common. Many successful women, from Arianna Huffington to Beyoncé, emphasize the importance of mental health in their personal success.

Arianna Huffington famously founded Thrive Global, a company dedicated to tackling burnout and promoting wellness, after her own wake-up call, where she collapsed from exhaustion. Her story teaches us that true wealth comes when you can operate at your best mentally.

Taking time for rest, meditation, and reflection can give you the clarity you need to make better financial decisions. It's not about being busy; it's about being intentional.

2. Physical Health as the Foundation for Financial Success

When you take care of your body, your mind and emotions follow. To build wealth, you need energy. Whether it's making decisions, closing deals, or executing your vision, your body needs to be strong. Serena Williams is a perfect example of someone who has built both physical and financial empires. As a world-class athlete, she knows that her health is the most important asset she can nurture.

Incorporate physical activity into your daily routine. Even if you're extremely busy, start small. Whether it's a walk, yoga, or a 15-minute morning stretch, you're investing in mental clarity and stress management, which will reflect in every area of your life, including your finances.

3. The Power of Saying No: Protecting Your Energy

Success often requires the ability to say no to distractions, commitments, and obligations that don't align with your goals. Learning this skill is just as important as the financial strategies you implement.

Take Reese Witherspoon, for example. As one of the highest-paid actresses in Hollywood, Reese shifted focus from being just an actor to creating her production company, Hello Sunshine. But she didn't do this at the cost of her health. She made strategic decisions about what to prioritize, knowing she couldn't do it all. She learned to protect her energy by saying no to certain projects that didn't align with her long-term vision.

4. Creating Rituals for Success

Developing daily rituals for your well-being can help you stay grounded, focused, and energized for the work ahead. Whether it's morning meditation, journaling your thoughts, or scheduling breaks throughout the day, these rituals can become the foundation of your success.

Michelle Obama, who balances her role as a mother, former First Lady, and successful author, incorporates a mix of exercise, family time, and personal reflection into her routine. These daily habits keep her balanced and give her the strength to achieve her goals.

5. The Role of Support Systems: Building Your Circle of Strength

No one builds wealth alone. Surround yourself with like-minded individuals who not only inspire you but also understand the balance between ambition and self-care. Oprah Winfrey has always surrounded herself with a powerful support system—her close-knit circle of friends, mentors, and advisors. They've helped her manage the pressures that come with massive success.

Find a network of supportive women who empower you to maintain your well-being while pursuing your dreams. Build communities that encourage rest, growth, and balance, and keep you on track for long-term success.

Bonus Section: "Wealth Building Resources: Tools You Can Use"

As you move forward in building your wealth, here are some practical tools that can help streamline the process, keep you on track, and provide valuable insight into your financial journey:

Mint (Budgeting Tool): Track your spending, set savings goals, and understand your finances in real-time.

Acorns (Investment Tool): Automatically invest spare change from everyday purchases and grow your wealth over time.

Robinhood (Stock Trading App): Start trading stocks and building your portfolio with zero commission fees.

Personal Capital (Financial Planning Tool): A comprehensive app to track your investments, budget, and long-term financial health.

Wealthfront (Automated Investment Service): Create a long-term wealth-building strategy with automated investments, tax-optimization, and portfolio management.

Practical Exercises for Sustaining Wealth

Exercise 1: Create Your Wealth Vision Board

Take some time to visualize your long-term financial goals. Create a vision board that incorporates not just your wealth, but your health, legacy, and values. Use images, words, and quotes that inspire you to stay focused on building wealth that serves your highest purpose.

Exercise 2: Develop Your Daily Self-Care Routine

Create a simple self-care routine that supports your financial journey. Whether it's a 10-minute meditation, a quick workout, or a few minutes of gratitude journaling, make sure your routine helps keep your mind clear and focused on what matters most.

Exercise 3: Review Your Financial Portfolio

Take a moment to review your current investments and savings. Are you diversified? Do you have a strategy for long-term growth? If not, create a plan to balance risk and reward, incorporating some of the lessons from this book.

integrate them into manuscript

Here's how we can integrate the bonus chapter and bonus sections into the manuscript. I'll add them directly after Chapter 4, expanding the narrative and offering added value to the reader:

Chapter 5: The Power of Wealth and Well-Being

In the hustle and bustle of our journey to financial independence, we often forget that true wealth isn't just about the numbers on our bank statements. It's about being whole— mentally, emotionally, and physically. This chapter brings together the ideas of self-care and financial success, showing that one feeds into the other. Just like the famous female entrepreneurs and leaders we admire—Arianna Huffington, Beyoncé, and Michelle Obama—they've all mastered the balance of working hard and taking care of themselves.

1. The Relationship Between Mental Health and Financial Success

Building wealth is tough, and it's often accompanied by stress, sleepless nights, and pressure. But mental health is just as crucial as the strategies you use to grow your finances. Think of Arianna Huffington, who found the limits of overworking and burnout, and built Thrive Global, a company that now emphasizes sleep and well-being. If you're constantly in "hustle mode," you're not operating at your highest potential. When you take care of your mind, you make clearer, smarter decisions. Remember that mental clarity leads to sound investments, better risk management, and increased creativity.

Exercise 1: Create Your Wealth Vision Board

Before jumping into the practicalities of wealth, take a step back and focus on your mind's vision of financial success. Create a vision board that doesn't just highlight wealth, but also emotional fulfillment, personal growth, and health. Surround yourself with visuals that remind you of the life you want to create—not just the material wealth.

2. Physical Health as the Foundation for Financial Success

If you think you can't be wealthy without sacrificing your health, think again. Some of the most successful women in the world, like Serena Williams, manage to balance their fitness routines with growing empires. Her mental strength, physical discipline, and stamina are the secret weapons behind her success. You can't achieve wealth if you're constantly fatigued or suffering from burnout. Integrate fitness into your daily life, whether it's yoga, walking, or even dance. Start small, but be consistent.

Exercise 2: Develop Your Daily Self-Care Routine

It's not just about financial routines—build a physical and mental self-care routine. It could be a morning stretch, a 10-minute meditation session, or a gratitude journal at night. The goal is to create moments in your day that refresh your mind and body, which in turn refreshes your approach to wealth-building.

3. The Power of Saying No: Protecting Your Energy

Saying no isn't a weakness; it's a superpower. Reese Witherspoon didn't become one of Hollywood's top stars by accepting every role thrown her way. She strategically said no to the opportunities that didn't align with her bigger vision. By saying no, you clear the path for things that truly matter—things that bring you growth, success, and fulfillment.

As you build your empire, protect your energy. Say no to distractions. Say no to toxic people. Say no to projects that don't resonate with your values or vision.

4. Creating Rituals for Success

Success doesn't happen overnight. It's built through daily actions, rituals, and consistency. Look at Michelle Obama, who, despite her chaotic schedule, finds time to exercise, reflect, and spend time with her family. Her rituals are part of her success. If you want to build lasting wealth, build rituals that support your vision.

These can be as simple as dedicating 15 minutes each morning to visualizing your goals, or setting aside an hour each week to review your financial goals.

5. The Role of Support Systems: Building Your Circle of Strength

Surround yourself with people who encourage and inspire you. Women like Oprah Winfrey didn't get to where they are alone. They surrounded themselves with a powerful support system—mentors, friends, and colleagues who understood their vision and lifted them up when needed. Build your own network of women who empower you to pursue your dreams. This community will provide not only advice and insight but also emotional support during challenging times.

Bonus Section: "Wealth-Building Resources: Tools You Can Use"

Building wealth requires the right tools. From budgeting to investing, there are countless resources available to help you stay on track. Here's a list of tools that will simplify your journey:

Mint (Budgeting Tool): Track your spending and savings with this easy-to-use app.

Acorns (Investment Tool): Start investing automatically with your spare change.

Robinhood (Stock Trading App): No commission fees, making stock trading more accessible.

Personal Capital (Financial Planning Tool): Get an overview of your portfolio and plan for the future.

Wealthfront (Automated Investment Service): Grow your wealth automatically, with minimal effort.

Practical Exercises for Sustaining Wealth

Exercise 3: Review Your Financial Portfolio

At least once a year, take the time to review your investments. Are you diversified? Are you making strategic moves toward your long-term goals? Make sure you're set up for growth, not just survival.

Exercise 4: Audit Your Time and Energy

Time is a form of currency too. Audit where your time is going. Are you spending it on things that bring you joy and wealth? If not, adjust accordingly. Wealth is built not just through money, but through the energy and time you invest in your priorities.

This section of the book aims to provide the reader with a holistic view of wealth—one that includes not just financial strategies but also personal health, energy management, and community building. As you move forward, these aspects of well-being will help you maintain a balanced approach to wealth-building, ensuring that the process is sustainable and fulfilling.

Chapter 6: Mastering the Money Game—Your Next Step Forward

As we look toward the next chapter, it's time to begin the final phase of your wealth journey: taking action and maintaining momentum. The previous chapters provided the foundation of a wealth-building mindset, but now you'll learn how to implement strategies that will bring it all to life.

With these integrations, we've built on the foundation laid in the previous chapters, bringing balance, practicality, and mental well-being into the fold. These additions ensure that the reader sees wealth not just as a financial goal but as a holistic pursuit that encompasses health, relationships, and mindset.

yes

Great! The manuscript is now more comprehensive, engaging, and inspiring. We've integrated both the foundational wealth-building strategies as well as elements of well-being and personal growth, which will make it resonate with a wide audience of ambitious women.

Leveraging Your Network: Relationships as Catalysts for Growth

The Art of Risk-Taking: How to Bet on Yourself

From Side Hustles to Full-Fledged Business: Turning Passion into Profit

Leaving a Legacy: Creating Wealth for Future Generations

Exciting Ending: Wealth Beyond Money – The Ultimate Fulfillment

Chapter 7: Leveraging Your Network: Relationships as Catalysts for Growth

Building wealth isn't just about mastering numbers and strategies—it's about relationships. The power of your network can elevate you to unimaginable heights, just as it did for women like Sara Blakely, the founder of Spanx, who credits her success to the relationships and mentors she cultivated throughout her career. Think of Sheryl Sandberg at Facebook, whose support system of like-minded women helped her rise to the top. Networking is your strategic asset.

1. Nurturing Meaningful Connections

When you surround yourself with people who inspire you, challenge you, and support your vision, you create an ecosystem of growth. Building these connections requires genuine relationships, not transactional ones. Look for mentors, peers, and collaborators who can bring different perspectives and skills to the table. Whether it's a business advisor, an accountant, or simply a group of like-minded women, the right people can unlock doors you never thought possible.

2. Taking Networking Beyond Business

Networking isn't just for the boardroom—it's also about building friendships, learning from others, and getting exposure to new ideas. Successful women like Oprah Winfrey didn't only rely on professional networks—they built personal bonds that fueled their growth. Attend networking events, but also invest time in connecting on a personal level. Relationships open up opportunities for collaboration, learning, and sharing resources.

Chapter 8: The Art of Risk-Taking: How to Bet on Yourself

In the journey of wealth-building, there comes a point when taking risks is not just necessary—it's the key to unlocking your next level of success. The most successful women in the world aren't afraid to bet on themselves, whether it's launching a new business, moving to a new city, or pivoting in their career. Richard Branson, Elon Musk, and Whitney Wolfe Herd (founder of Bumble) all took calculated risks that reshaped their futures.

1. The Fear of Failure and How to Overcome It

Fear of failure is one of the most common barriers to taking risks. But what many women fail to realize is that failure isn't the end—it's often the beginning of something greater. Learning from your mistakes and using them as stepping stones is how wealth is built. Successful risk-takers know that the biggest opportunities often lie just beyond comfort zones.

2. Calculated Risks vs. Reckless Decisions

While it's important to take risks, it's equally important to take calculated risks. Oprah Winfrey once said, "Do what you feel in your heart to be right—for you'll be criticized anyway." That's not reckless; it's about having a plan and understanding the potential outcomes. Do your research, talk to mentors, and ensure that the risk you're taking aligns with your long-term vision.

Chapter 9: From Side Hustles to Full-Fledged Business: Turning Passion into Profit

At some point, many women start with a side hustle—something they're passionate about and do on the side for extra income. But how do you turn that passion into a full-fledged business? The key lies in turning your hobbies and interests into something scalable and sustainable. Sophia Amoruso, the founder of Nasty Gal, started her business by selling vintage clothes on eBay before turning it into a billion-dollar fashion empire. Your passion is your foundation.

1. Identifying Your Niche and Market

Start by understanding your strengths and what you can offer the market. Is it a product, a service, or perhaps a digital offering like an online course? Knowing your niche and your audience will help you carve out a place in the market where you can thrive.

2. Scaling Your Business

Once your side hustle gains traction, the next step is scaling it up. This can be through hiring a team, launching an online store, or creating new products. But scaling isn't just about growth—it's about sustainable growth. The process of scaling requires thoughtful planning and strategic investments, whether it's marketing, technology, or operations.

Chapter 10: Leaving a Legacy: Creating Wealth for Future Generations

One of the most powerful aspects of wealth-building is that it allows you to create a legacy—a lasting impact that goes beyond your lifetime. This isn't just about passing down money; it's about passing down values, opportunities, and resources to the next generation. Think of women like Melinda Gates, whose work is dedicated to philanthropy, education, and empowering future generations.

1. Teaching Financial Literacy to the Next Generation

It's important to impart financial literacy to your children or younger people in your community. Teach them the principles of managing money, investing, and understanding their financial choices. By doing this, you're giving them the tools to continue the wealth-building process for generations to come.

2. Giving Back and Creating Impact

As you build wealth, think about how you can give back to others. Philanthropy, mentorship, and creating opportunities for those less fortunate are powerful ways to leave a legacy. Rihanna, for example, didn't just create a business empire with Fenty Beauty—she also created the Clara Lionel Foundation, empowering women and children worldwide. Wealth is most fulfilling when it's used to create positive change.

Exciting Ending: Wealth Beyond Money – The Ultimate Fulfillment

As we come to the end of this journey, it's important to remember that true wealth isn't measured solely by the amount of money in your bank account. It's about having the freedom to live life on your own terms, the power to make choices that align with your values, and the fulfillment of creating something meaningful that will last.

Building wealth is a powerful act, but the act of giving back, helping others, and becoming a beacon of light for those who need it most is the ultimate form of success. The wealthiest women in the world—whether in business, in philanthropy, or in life—understand that the more they share and empower others, the greater their legacy will be.

Your next step?

Go out and create the world you want. Build your wealth, build your empire, and never stop believing in your own power. You are not just building financial freedom—you are crafting a life full of impact, purpose, and, yes, unimaginable wealth.

This expanded content brings depth and a sense of purpose to the wealth-building journey. It not only covers the practical steps but also focuses on fulfillment, legacy, and the bigger picture of wealth, creating a well-rounded experience for readers.

add some more information not chapterwise

Absolutely! Let's add some more actionable insights, strategies, and personal growth principles to enhance the manuscript, providing more depth and enriching the reader's experience. Here are some additional sections that integrate both practical wealth-building strategies and the mindset needed to achieve lasting success:

The Power of Belief: Rewriting Your Money Story

One of the most significant obstacles women face on their journey to wealth is their own beliefs about money. The narrative we tell ourselves about money, wealth, and our place in the world directly impacts our ability to accumulate wealth. Oprah Winfrey, for example, grew up in poverty, but she rewrote her story, believing that she could create opportunities not just for herself, but for others as well.

1. Challenging Limiting Beliefs

Women often grow up with societal beliefs that tell them wealth is a man's domain or that they should be humble and not talk about money. These beliefs are limiting, and often, they are inherited. You can rewrite your money story by challenging these outdated beliefs and replacing them with affirmations of abundance, confidence, and the knowledge that you deserve wealth just as much as anyone else.

Start by identifying your limiting beliefs about money. Do you think you're not good with numbers? Or that money is hard to make? These beliefs may stem from your past, but they don't define your future. As you begin to challenge these beliefs, you'll open up new doors to financial freedom.

2. Abundance vs. Scarcity Mindset

The abundance mindset believes there is enough for everyone, that there is always room for more success and wealth. In contrast, the scarcity mindset often creates a competitive, fear-based view of the world—where success and wealth are limited resources. A scarcity mindset may convince you that there are only so many opportunities, and if someone else wins, there is less for you.

To move toward abundance, start seeing wealth as something that grows exponentially— and the more people who experience it, the more it benefits society as a whole. Remember, someone else's success is not your failure. Women supporting women is a fundamental part of wealth creation and emotional fulfillment. The wealth-building journey is not about fighting for the last spot; it's about creating a path where everyone can win.

The Importance of Self-Care in Wealth-Building

Many women strive for success but often neglect their mental, emotional, and physical well-being. You cannot truly build wealth if you don't take care of yourself. Your energy, focus, and clarity of mind are your greatest assets. Think of Arianna Huffington, who has spoken about the importance of sleep and self-care in achieving long-term success. She even stepped down from her role at The Huffington Post to prioritize her well-being and explore wellness initiatives.

1. Energy Management Over Time Management

Instead of focusing solely on time management, consider focusing on energy management. Wealth-building can be exhausting, and it often requires long hours, high levels of focus, and emotional resilience. That's why it's essential to keep your energy reserves high.

Some practical tips for managing energy:

Practice mindfulness: Meditation, yoga, and even just deep breathing can help rejuvenate your mind and body, keeping you sharp.

Sleep is non-negotiable: Get enough rest to ensure that your brain functions optimally. Studies have shown that lack of sleep can drastically reduce productivity and creativity.

Healthy eating and exercise: Fueling your body with nutritious food and regular physical activity enhances your physical and mental stamina, making you more capable of handling the demands of building wealth.

2. Create Your Own Rituals of Success

Having personal rituals helps you stay grounded and keeps your success on track. Whether it's a morning routine, journaling about your goals, or setting aside quiet time to reflect on your progress, these practices provide clarity and a strong foundation for achieving your wealth-building goals. Self-care rituals foster a positive mindset, reduce stress, and give you the emotional strength to handle setbacks.

The Power of Financial Education

Women who succeed in building wealth are relentless about their financial education. This is a key differentiator. Successful women, like Suze Orman, Elizabeth Warren, and Warren Buffett, all emphasize the importance of understanding money—how it works, how to grow it, and how to protect it.

1. Educate Yourself About Money Management

You don't need to become a financial expert overnight, but you should become familiar with the basics:

Budgeting

Saving

Investing

Credit management

Understanding taxes

The more knowledgeable you become about managing your finances, the more confident you'll feel about making decisions that will accelerate your wealth-building journey. There are plenty of resources—books, podcasts, and online courses—that can teach you financial literacy.

2. Investing is Key

Investing is one of the most powerful tools for building wealth over time. Women, however, tend to underinvest compared to men, often due to fear or lack of knowledge. You don't have to be an expert in the stock market to start investing. Begin by researching low-cost index funds or speaking with a financial advisor who can help you determine an investment strategy that fits your goals.

Billionaire investor Mellody Hobson once said, "The biggest risk of all is not taking one." When you invest, you are making your money work for you. The earlier you start, the greater the compound interest. In fact, women tend to be better long-term investors because they approach it with patience and discipline.

The Role of Giving Back: Building Wealth With Purpose

Wealth is not just about accumulation; it's about purpose and impact. Many successful women, like Melinda Gates, are using their wealth to make a difference. The key to ultimate wealth is finding a balance between financial gain and contributing to something bigger than yourself.

1. Giving Creates Abundance

When you share your wealth—whether it's through donations, mentorship, or supporting causes that matter—you create a cycle of abundance. Your wealth will not only help you live a fulfilling life, but it will also have a ripple effect, empowering others to do the same. Whether it's funding a scholarship, helping a friend start a business, or supporting a charity, giving back aligns your wealth with your values.

Conclusion: Creating a Life of Wealth and Purpose

Building wealth is an incredible journey, and the wealth you create is only as meaningful as the impact it has on the world around you. As you develop your millionaire mindset and take actionable steps toward your financial goals, remember that wealth is not just about numbers—it's about purpose, passion, and impact.

True fulfillment comes from knowing that you are not only securing a better future for yourself but also empowering others along the way. By redefining wealth on your terms—embracing your vision, taking bold risks, and building meaningful relationships—you will become a beacon of what's possible for women everywhere.

As you take the final steps on this transformative journey, remember: wealth is not a destination; it's a way of living. By embracing these principles and continuing to grow in every aspect of your life, you will build the kind of wealth that lasts for generations—and brings you true happiness and purpose.

Top of Form

Bottom of Form

www.ingramcontent.com/pod-product-compliance
Lightning Source LLC
Chambersburg PA
CBHW040211110726
48005CB00019B/2974